FR McDYER
OF GLENCOLUMBKILLE

AN AUTOBIOGRAPHY

BRANDON

First paperback edition 1984
Brandon Book Publishers Ltd
Dingle, Co. Kerry, Ireland

© *Father James McDyer 1982*

ISBN 0 86322 053 3

Cover design: Brendan Foreman
Typesetting: Gifford & Craven
Printed by Biddles Ltd, Guildford, England

ACKNOWLEDGEMENTS

For research, advice and encouragement, the author wishes to thank Francis Cunningham, Liam Cunningham, Mary Anne Gillespie, Colum Kenny, Deirdre McCartin, Steve MacDonogh, Bernie Melvor and John Meehan.

DEDICATION

To the Irish people at home and abroad

PREFACE

Every life has its meaning. Mine sometimes seems to me a mere kaleidoscope of events and impressions in which the passage of time is a single instant. The person struggling through the business of some meeting with government officials is also the child preparing mischief. And the meaning of a life can have as much to do with the people and experiences encountered along the way as anything innate in character.

I hope that this account may have meaning for many of its readers of a kind which they can use. I have my own conclusions, of course, but the most important are those which readers draw for themselves. The achievements, disappointments, successes and failures are set down so that people can make of them what they will.

If I have learned nothing else from my life, I have learned from the start about the effects of oppression and neglect in the West of Ireland. In my own way, I have worked to counter those effects, so that my dream of a Glencolumbkille rescued from the decay for which history seemed to have destined it, has been largely fulfilled.

What I have learned impels me in a new direction. Perhaps it is some kind of restless will, or vanity even, that makes me unwilling to relax into the "dignified" passivity that seems to be expected of my age.

Dreams of freedom, of the ability of people to take power into their own hands to build a fully human future, know no boundaries. So now, translating dream into practice, I plan to assist some other community far away which faces simi-

7

lar problems to those we faced in Glencolumbkille thirty years ago.

In Latin America people are combining in communal enterprise to combat rural deprivation. They are seeking to build independent prosperity on their own terms through shared efforts out of backgrounds of poverty inherited from centuries of political neglect and oppression.

I do not say that mine was the best or only way. Also, I am a product of my times and circumstances; new generations and new circumstances will surely — and must — yield new and better solutions.

James McDyer, P.P.
Carrick
26 February 1982

CHAPTER I

The most indelible impression of my childhood and adolescence was what was called in Donegal "the convoy" or *comoradh*. Convoys were the gatherings of neighbours in the homes of those about to emigrate, in order to wish them a last farewell on their trip to America, Australia, or New Zealand. They were a constant feature of life towards the end of the nineteenth and the beginning of the twentieth century.

The pathos and the poignancy of these occasions were beyond belief. This was not the departure of people who would return soon again, for in those days of slow travel it was recognised that it would be many years before emigrants would be able to undertake the long journey back to their homeland if, indeed, they ever came back again.

This was not the sorrow of an Irish wake where grief is confined usually to the passing of some elderly relative who has gone to his God. This was the passing from the community of someone who was young and vibrant, someone who was leaving a land which, though often rugged and poor, was deeply beloved.

The convoy started on the night before departure, in the emigrant's home. It commenced on a gay note, but gaiety did not run very deep. The tears and the sadness were just below the surface. The fiddlers arrived; the kitchen was cleared for the dance; the neighbours arrived, and the dance commenced. The old father and mother carried out their usual courtesies of welcome and hospitality but as the night advanced into morning, you would often surprise the mother wiping away a quiet tear, or you might awaken "himself" from a deep reverie over the peaty fire.

In most cases there was the added wrench of the emigrant from a sweetheart whom he or she would probably never see again. The songs would be sung between the dances, and it was not unknown for the emigrants to break down in the middle of their own contributions. Women would quietly weep, and men would cough in embarrassment, or move out into the morning air.

Suddenly it was dawn; the last few odds and ends were hastily packed. The fiddlers put their instruments away. The neighbours moved out to the street as if by common consent that these last few moments be left in privacy to the people of the household and the departing exile.

Then the emigrant emerged. Handshakes all around. Men held their grief and covered up in gruff silence. Women seized their aprons and dabbed their eyes. Down the boreen, or lane, the procession went; the last farewells on the country road were followed by the walk to the nearest railway station accompanied by a younger brother, a sweetheart, and one or two friends.

At a bend in the road the emigrant would turn and keep waving to the little knot of people left behind, until he could be seen no longer. Then the last wave of farewell. The father would enter the house to brood over the fire; the mother would sit out on a rock beyond the cabbage garden, and remain seated there for hours gazing in the direction in which her child had gone.

It is small wonder that this kindly rural people, who were so attached to their homeland, felt that life was full of partings and tears. It is small wonder that they somehow felt cheated of the opportunity to carve their own destiny in their own land, but they had come to accept emigration with the same stoicism with which they accepted sickness or death.

* * *

I am quite sure that the earliest influences of home and environment deeply affect the character of the future citizen and man. I suppose the home into which I was born in 1910 would be classified as a good one: it had an aura of respectability comparable with most of the other homes around. The community — or townland, as it was called — was the townland of Kilraine, near the village of Glenties in West Donegal. The Glenties area is like an enormous basin, or a saucer surrounded by mountains; and I used to think that our large valley was the whole world. All the residents were small farmers with an average size farm of about thirty acres. They were not the poorest of the poor in Donegal, but by no standard could any of them be considered rich.

My parents, John and Brigid McDyer, were exceedingly hard-working, but like all our neighbours they were ever ready to lend the helping hand to some neighbour who was ill, or to join in a *meitheal* when some homestead had lost its breadwinner. Indeed, my mother must have been considered an unofficial midwife at a time when there was no district nurse, and whenever we children saw her make up a special parcel of clothes, together with the very special apron, and inform us that she was going to visit a neighbour woman who was ill, we kept solemn faces. Little did she know of the giggles that took place after her departure, for we well knew what her mission was. Little did she suspect the sense of freedom that prevailed, for during the next twenty-four hours there would be home rule!

But these periods of freedom were short-lived for me, because the anarchy which at first prevailed quickly gave place to an oligarchy among the older members of the family who restrained juniors with a firm hand. And unfortunately, I was at the end of the line. Senior to me were Minnie, Jack, Charlie, Hugh, Philomena, and Alec. My father never interfered. Usually he was out working in the farmyard or on the farm. Anyhow, he was a jovial type and rarely exercised discipline. It would seem that by mutual consent such a chore was allotted to my mother. She could not tolerate idleness, and her motto seemed to be that the busy child would have no time for mischief. Chores were already planned for the after-school hours, and for Saturdays, and we all had our allotted tasks, however light. I was usually regarded as hopeless in the discharge of these jobs, because I was much more attracted to reading than to helping on the farm, and when I

11

was given a job to do I usually made a mess of it and used my imagination to create some form of mischief instead.

Our house contained one double bedroom, four single bedrooms, a sitting room, and the kitchen which, with its great turf fire, was the centre of the home. The farm included both crops and livestock, and I was greatly attached to our horse called Paddy. My father used to be wild with me for giving him sugar; and when I came home from college the first thing I would do would be to go out to see Paddy; as I approached him he would prance about, recognising my voice or smell, I suppose.

No Irish was spoken in our home. My father spoke Irish well, having inherited it from his parents who were native speakers. But unfortunately my mother, who came from Inishowen, could not speak a word of Irish. It was the people of my father's generation who gradually relinquished the use of Irish in my native district.

I read much, even when I was supposed to be working, and even in those childhood days I had my heroes and I dreamed of how I could imitate their prowess. They were a strange assortment. First there was Cuchulainn, the legendary hero of Ulster who, single-handed, with efficiency and courage alone routed an army. Then there was Christ, whose qualities of tolerance, compassion, innocence and courage, compelled my admiration. And finally, there was Terence McSwiney — a supreme example of physical and moral courage. And also, Michael Collins and Cathal Brugha, who thrilled the Irish people in my childhood by their feats of daring. These were my heroes, and I am sure they exerted a powerful influence on my child mind, as I fretted over work that was planned for me, and I longed for the day when some kind of self-determination would be within my grasp.

In addition to being lazy and carefree, I was extremely prankish. Of course, in a happy and healthy home such as ours, almost every one of us children was mischievous, but I think that in the planning and execution of a well-hatched scheme to bring about the discomfiture of others, I was regarded as the supreme pest. A home has a hierarchical structure, and as I was the youngest member, I felt I must do

12

something to level the imbalance.

Looking back on it all, I reckon that I was gifted with a fertile imagination. I would study weaknesses; I would carefully assess how these could be assailed; I would sift the various options; I would plan the timing and then I would act. Sometimes I would require help in the execution, and my brother, Alec, was a willing accomplice. This same brother has often told me since how all of the family became suspicious if they saw me sitting in deep thought and chuckling to myself. In such circumstances they all became alert.

Religion played a prominent part in our home. Looking back on it now after the passage of sixty years, it was not so much the practice of family prayers or the attendance at Mass on Sundays which had the greatest influence on us all. It was the pervading deep conviction of our parents that we were on this world for a short time, and that life did not end with the grave. I think that my mother with her punctilious attention to prayers had less influence on me than the deep-seated belief of my father. Life had no meaning for him if at the end of its hard-fought struggle there was no reward. With him it was a conviction which could not be explained by education — he had only an elementary education anyhow, — but it was so deep-seated that it permeated his whole life and governed his actions and his hopes.

Sunday was the one day when we all gathered for the midday meal. It took the form almost of a weekly general meeting. My mother went to great trouble to provide an attractive meal on a limited budget. It was the one day in the week when we were certain to have a four-course dinner with meat. It was the one day when we ate baker's bread, which was considered a great treat by us youngsters. All the other household bread was baked by my mother.

Conversation at the meal often resolved into a pep-talk about education, and time and again we were reminded that our parents were in no position to leave a legacy behind them, but that they would try to give each of us a second-level education, and after that it would remain with ourselves to chart our own courses.

13

There was no radio or television in those days, so we were left to our own devices to create entertainment. Sunday afternoons were almost always devoted to football. In the summer we would hunt salmon in the local river, or trout in the lakes. Indeed, I recall that often during the Sunday sermon at Mass I spent my time planning the fishing programme for that afternoon.

The harvest fair day in the village of Glenties was an annual landmark. How we looked forward to it for weeks before, for it seemed to us that the whole world assembled in Glenties on that day! How we watched with growing excitement the drovers drive their sheep and cattle, and even flocks of geese, along the road on the evening before! How we boasted to each other about the number of shillings we had accumulated as spending money!

For us, the attractions of the harvest fair were not the trading of livestock. Oh no! There were more attractive things still, and they were the seemingly innumerable stalls with games of chance and skill. Stalls selling dulce (or dilisk); stalls selling crab apples; stalls selling cures for rheumatism and all kinds of cures for all kinds of diseases.

I can still see the stall-holders with their red noses; their jaunty caps perched at angles; and their loud voices grown raucous over the years with constant shouting. I can hear their bawdy jokes, and woe betide you if you asked them some innocent question, for they would hold you up to ridicule which would send you scurrying into the anonymity of the crowd.

But now their forum roars no longer. Many of the tents will never again be unfolded, and the harvest fair day is but a pale replica of its former diversity. Now the business of buying and selling rules the day.

It is not nostalgia to say we have lost something: we must face up to the fact that the evolution of our "civilisation" cannot be assumed to mean progress. We have lost something when we cease to interact; when we cease to come together in groups to enrich each other's lives; to stimulate; to rely upon our wit and our spirit; to inspire and support each other.

The day of the haystack was another great day, when seventeen or eighteen men would assemble to cart in the hay and build it in a stack, which they also thatched and roped. I suppose the most lasting impression that the day of the haystack left on me was the coming together of a group of men to do a day's work in their community, without pay. The offering of money to any of these men would have been considered an insult. Instead, there was an implicit gentleman's agreement that if you had a group of men to help you, then you in turn would be expected to give a day's labour to each of them in return.

How I remember the men and horses gather in the morning just as we were leaving for school, and the scarcely concealed hierarchy of the various participants. High on the list of the skilled were the men who built the loads on the carts, and great was the pride of him who could build the largest load. The men who forked the hay to the builders were in a category by themselves, and great was the envy of their strength and brawn.

But of course the building of the large haystack was reserved for those who considered themselves the élite in craftsmanship, and so great was their self-esteem that they would brook no criticism. However, the ultimate accolade in skill was reserved for the thatchers. These were a few of the most elderly, and woe betide any of the younger set who intruded on their domain.

As I reflect on these intriguing distinctions, it is clear that these people from rural parts who had been neglected for many generations, and were classified by the haughty élite as mere peasants, felt an inward compulsion to assert their dignity and their skills, and compete against each other.

As evening wore on and the work was completed, a fiddler would arrive, some drink would be bought, and a hard day's work would be concluded with merriment and dancing.

My mother always endeavoured to make much of the traditional Irish feasts, like Christmas, St. Bridget's Eve, Shrove Tuesday, St. Patrick's Day, Easter, and All Hallows Eve. A linen cloth would cover the table; a candle would be lighted in the centre, and the best meals of the year would be served with the traditional dishes of the occasion.

After the meal at Christmas, or at Easter, the family concert would be held and each of us was supposed to contribute. My mother, though musical, never sang, but my father sang quite well and did so often, while he was at work, and I distinctly remember my feeling of pride when I taught him a rebel song called "Kevin Barry". On other feasts we would play a game of cards or blind man's buff, in which we all took part.

These occasions left a lasting impression on me. They complemented my experiences of our small rural community working together. But the family entertainments were the microcosm of the community; the family united around the festive board with the lighted candle in our midst, which my mother told us represented Christ. They were great experiences, and they have always represented to me the importance of the cell of all society.

CHAPTER II

I hated school; and I think every child of my generation did likewise. I do not know whether this detestation emanated from the regimentation of one's day, or from the strict and sometimes harsh discipline which endeavoured to ensure that you worked and did not talk, or from the limited opportunities for recreation — or from a combination of all these.

Ours was a country school, built alongside the main road, with a catchment area of about one and a half miles. We went barefooted to school from April until summer holidays in order to save the shoes, and ease the constrictions of the family budget. The heating was supplied by ourselves and each pupil carried two sods of turf to school each morning during the winter. There was no hot cocoa. Instead, each of us carried two pieces of oaten cake joined together with country butter. This was our lunch.

The solid squat building, with a prominent porch which bore the sign "Erected in 1873", was typical of the national schools of that time. In the porch was a wash-basin; an open cloak-room; and a partitioned section for the sods of turf.

Inside, there was the classroom undivided by any partition where a principal teacher and a junior assistant mistress were compelled to compete with each other in the pitch of their voices.

Ranged in the rear half of the room were twelve long desks, in batches of three, and each desk was capable of accommodating about seven pupils. As they sat in the desks the pupils were confronted by two teacher's desks and two blackboards. The only decorations on the walls were a map

17

of Ireland, a map of the British Isles, a small blackboard with the day's attendance marked on it in numerals, and a map of the world with the British possessions marked in red.

One large fire surrounded by a fire-guard supplied the heat, but as this did not reach the back desks, a concession was granted whereby four or five pupils in turn could come to the fire for a short period to warm their hands.

Short trousers to the knees, a *gansey* and a coat were worn by the boys who, like the girls, wore long black stockings held just under the knees by an elastic band. The girls' skirts extended well below the knees and were usually made of Donegal homespun, like the boys' pants. Almost all the girls wore their hair in plaits — either single or double plaits. Girls never had their hair cut in those days.

It was at the national school that I first began to figure out some of the great differences between boys and girls. My estimate was that girls were much more civilised than boys. Boys were ostentatious and extrovert and loud-mouthed, caring for nobody but themselves. Girls were much more conscientious and more assiduous. This often placed us in a bad light, and consequently we would try to even the score by squirting ink over their copy-books, or slyly pull the pig-tail of the girl in the long desk in front. As the girl turned around to protest, she would find her tormentor apparently working industriously, and in the ensuing hullabaloo, the poor girl would be blamed by the teacher.

In the long years that have passed since then, I have never changed my opinion about the respective levels of civilisation possessed by the female and the male.

The school curriculum in my early days was much the same as it is today, but two or three subjects have long since been abandoned. Probably the most important of these was a subject which we called "Latin roots", wherein the senior children were taught how to correlate much of our spoken language with the Latin language with which it has such kinship. The presence of Latin in our studies really carried on a tradition from previous generations when the native Irish were banned from education and resorted to the "hedge school" where the illegal teachers actually imparted a good

18

knowledge not only of Latin but of Greek as well.

So, although our own language had been pushed into the background, I think that the link with long traditions through the learning of Latin not only had a broadening effect but also imparted a deep sense of identity with our Irish heritage.

My national school period bridged the transition from the British régime to the régime of the Irish Free State. During the British régime the Irish language was taught — but as an extra subject and outside the normal school hours. Our teacher, who was an enthusiast for the Irish language, made full use of this facility, but we children who were compelled to remain for one half-hour after closing time, did not quite share this enthusiasm.

Looking back, it is easy now to see how this method served to distort childhood attitudes and to weaken our interest in our own inheritance. However, my experience was a far cry from the days when my father went to school for, according to his story, children were actually beaten by the teacher if they were discovered speaking Irish.

But if life at the school was hum-drum, it certainly was enlivened in my time by the War of Independence, which had its origins in the 1916 Rebellion, and which really hotted up in 1919.

In December 1918 a general election was held for the whole of the "United Kingdom" of Great Britain and Ireland, the electorate of the whole island of Ireland voting over-whelmingly for independence. Sinn Féin carried seventy-three seats, the Unionists twenty-six, and others six.

The following month, on 21 January 1919, the Sinn Féin representatives constituted themselves as an all-Ireland parliament in Dublin. This was the first Dáil: it was quickly outlawed by the British who were then opposed in arms by the Irish Volunteers.

The British, in addition to their ordinary soldiery, poured in thousands of that very extraordinary type known as the Black and Tans because of the colour of their uniforms. They were not really soldiers in that they were a special force of, for the Irish, undesirables who were recruited to put down

19

rebellion in whatever way was deemed necessary. They cartainly had little discipline. Naturally, as Irish school-children, our sympathies were entirely with the Irish Volunteers.

As we gathered together at play-time and heard the results of the latest encounter between the Irish Volunteers and the British, we would raise a cheer if our people had scored a victory during an engagement. To us it was like a football match where we cheered lustily if the home team was winning.

Nevertheless, this was not entirely an indication of the callousness of youth. Our feelings also stemmed from the history we learned, and from the traditions handed down from father to son about the disgraceful treatment of our people meted out by successive British governments.

My earliest recollection of the Anglo-Irish war of 1919-22 was on a night when the barracks in the neighbouring village of Glenties was being attacked. The Irish Volunteers had cut the road outside our home to prevent British reinforcements arriving. Two late travellers stumbled on the operation and were promptly jailed in our house, complete with a guard, until morning. My mother thought we children were all asleep, but she was horrified to learn later that we had been crowding the bedroom windows all night to watch the action.

I remember returning from Mass on a Sunday with adults, and as we walked along the country road, we met three Crossley tenders driven at break-neck speed, and filled with British forces. They felt frustrated that the congregation had dispersed before they could round them up and search them, and so they vented their fury by leaning out of their vehicles attempting to club us with their gun-butts. Had they but known it there was no better way to weld the Irish people into an army.

The last engagement of that war took place about three hundred yards from our house. We were sitting at dinner when we suddenly heard the staccato sound of rifles being fired, followed by the screaming sound of an overworked engine as the British Crossley tender fled for cover. We rushed out and saw the Volunteers fighting their retreat up the hillside. The British evacuated their tender and took up positions to retaliate. How we wished that they would fail. The British suffered one casualty who, as he lay on the road before he died, emptied his revolver through the windows of the nearest house.

In their frustration the British returned that evening and shot up the nearby village of Glenties, and indeed it was well for us that the Anglo-Irish Truce was declared a few days later, for the British, as was their custom, had earmarked for burning the houses in the immediate vicinity of the engagement.

But the war ended in 1922, and part of Ireland was amputated despite the declared wish of the Irish people in the ballot box in 1918.

I inherited my strong sense of nationalism from my own father, who himself witnessed some of the worst effects of evictions by British landlords. And his father, in turn, had passed on to him the feelings of outrage when the Irish were allowed to die in their hundreds of thousands during the Great Famine of 1847.

And after the passage of a lifetime, as I review more rationally our history over the period of hundreds of years of British occupation, my own feeling of outrage has not changed much. Of course, I abjure violence of any kind. But I say to myself again and again, "Why do they not leave us in peace and go back to their own country?"

We have no quarrel with the British people. They are decent and fair. But in their name successive British governments have wrought the most untold misery on our island people.

Since the first British army arrived in Ireland, there has been violence, bloodshed, death, persecution, hatred, deprivation, poverty, and exile. They banned the education of the Irish, and then they sneered at us for our ignorance; they outlawed our religion and they hunted our priests down like dogs; and perhaps the greatest and most enduring indignity of all — they cleared the Irish from large tracts of their native soil and, cuckoo-like, planted their hostile colonist egg in our lark's nest.

For us who lived in the county of Donegal, the partitioning of Ireland was humiliating and exasperating. Naturally, we were overjoyed that we belonged to that part of Ireland which was formally independent. But as part of the province of Ulster, which had traditionally asserted its independence of the British, it grieved us that six of the counties of our province still remained under the British crown.

Moreover, Donegal was now almost a geographical and political island because only one main road linked it with the other counties of our state.

I remember even as a young boy, the sense of deflation when the Truce was called. I felt cheated then and I have felt cheated ever since, that a minority in our island could dictate the destiny of our land. I resolved that if ever the opportunity arose I would work indefatigably for the good of our people.

* * *

In school-days, too, I was awakening to the customs, traditions and social life of the community in which we lived. In the winter-time there was hardly ever a dull night. On most nights a few of the neighbours would call. It was a *céilí*, or as it was known in Donegal, "a night's raking". The discussions at these gatherings ranged from weather, live-stock, illnesses, through to politics, and eventually finished off — presumably for the entertainment of the children — with fairy stories and ghost stories. I remember sitting spell-bound through these stories. Everybody was quite vocal. Not one of the neighbours could claim to be very advanced in learning and yet the imagery of their language, the apt choice of phrase, the descriptive detail, and the perfection of suspense in the telling of a story was something that much more educated people could rarely attain. Moreover, each one of these visitors had a highly distinctive personality which was honed and refined in an age when people were required to entertain each other.

I remember Paddy well! He lived up on the hillside; and he could turn his hand to anything. Not only was he a farmer, a stone mason and a cobbler, but on the occasion of

a country dance he could take the fiddle and give a commen-
dable rendering of Irish jigs, reels, hornpipes or traditional
airs. Gruff in manner, and blunt in speech, he had nevertheless a heart of gold, and many a neighbour could testify to
his willing help at times of distress or failure. We as children
often sat entranced as he recounted in the minutest detail his
youthful escapades with my father in eluding the landlord's
bailiffs when as young men they had poached salmon from
the nearby river. Of course the poaching of salmon was
regarded in those days as fair practice because the owner of
the river was a landlord with an English background.

Frank, whose home was in a hollow between the hills, was
a completely different personality, I remember. He spoke so
loudly you'd have thought he was addressing a public
meeting. Indeed, though we lived almost a mile from his
farm, we often heard every word of his conversation with
another farmer who worked in the fields beyond. He had the
reputation of being extremely thrifty. Not one square yard,
not one stalk of potatoes or piece of straw on his farm was
allowed to go to waste. His utilisation of every last scrap of
available resources made a lasting impression on me. The
dividing line between poverty and relative security was a very
slender line indeed. It was even related uncharitably of him
that he had a special pipe capable of carrying an ounce of
tobacco which he only carried to wakes and haystack days
where the tobacco was free.

The story was told about his marriage which took place
many years before my schooldays. Through shyness, but
also perhaps because of parsimoniousness, his marriage was
so secretly arranged that nobody knew except the old parish
priest, two trusted witnesses, and, of course, the bride. But
somehow, a leakage took place at the last moment and the
local young turks whom he hoped would be excluded from
the act, were determined to embarrass him. They appeared
in strength just as the old parish priest was opening the book
and adjusting his spectacles to begin the ceremony. As was
the custom of the time, all and sundry crowded around the
bride and groom, quite close to the contracting parties. On
this particular occasion one of them was not especially

23

comradely, for he placed himself immediately behind Frank and he was armed with a long pin. Just as Frank opened his mouth to utter the irrevocable affirmative, the corker pin was vigorously applied to the softest part of his rear anatomy and instead of announcing the usual words of consent, Frank gave utterance to the groan of a man in deep pain. The old parish priest assumed that Frank was just nervous and overcome by the occasion, so he asked the question a second time. Just as Frank proceeded to reply again, the corker pin was applied with added vigour and probably struck the bone, because Frank's reply was not a mere groan this time but a piercing yell. I never did hear, when the wedding was finally contracted, whether Frank's tormentor was a guest at the reception.

My father, himself, was full of humour and often matched the stories of visiting raconteurs with a vividness and a humour all his own. He told us of Jimmy, who was in the prime of manhood when my father was a young man. Jimmy was a man of powerful physique, great eloquence, and broad vision. He was a convinced Parnellite. Jimmy was so eloquent and gesticulated so much that it was considered a minor hazard to walk the road with him to Mass or market, because he became so agitated that he vehemently punched the shoulders of anyone beside him; it often became safer to walk along the fence and allow Jimmy the middle of the road to punch the air instead!

When Jimmy was a young man he was convicted of striking a landlord's bailiff during a nocturnal salmon poaching foray on the local river. Those were the days when landlordism was anathema to Irish country people, and Jimmy was chief local advocate of Home Rule. His violent assault on the bailiff actually rescued a colleague poacher who had just been seized. This immediately raised Jimmy to the status of a local hero. He was sent to gaol in Derry for six months, and when he was freed, he was greeted by a massive popular reception.

Naturally, Jimmy spoke from an outdoor platform, and spoke at length, and his speech ranged over many a subject. But, since fresh groups of people kept enlarging the throng,

24

he addressed the crowd in three or four further speeches. I often heard my father say that at about three a.m. or thereabouts, when Jimmy stood on a chair to make his eleventh speech, nobody could hear him because his voice had become so hoarse.

These were some of the experiences and customs of my childhood in Glenties some sixty years ago. A new generation with a new script acts out the drama of life today with new customs and new conventions. But through it all, the unedited manuscript of God remains etched indelibly on our mountains, lakes, and rivers, in all its immutable glory.

The dawn orchestra of the birds still exhilarates on a spring morning there with the timeless harmony of thousands of years. The dandelion, the celandine, the woodbine, the wild orchid and the humble daisy sparkle along the banks of the Owenea river and dance merrily in the breeze. The same pools are still there where we bathed and caught trout and salmon.

Binn Mor with inscrutable face and wide-flung arms looks down on the changing people in the valley below. The sun still rises behind distant Achla mountain, and disappears each evening behind the steeps of Sliabh a Tooey, sending up multi-coloured shafts of light from a raft of clouds as if waving farewell to the people until another day shall dawn.

CHAPTER III

It is rarely appreciated nowadays that fifty or sixty years ago there were few outlets of second level education in rural Ireland. And moreover, secondary education was not free. It involved sacrifice on the part of most parents to give their children its advantages. In my own case when I reached the usual starting age there was not enough money to send me to secondary school, and so I was delayed a year.

Actually in the whole county of Donegal at that time there were only two second-level schools for boys, and one for girls. There was only one boarding school for boys — St. Eunan's College in Letterkenny — and it was owned by the Catholic Church which hoped that it would be a preparatory college for the priesthood. However, after the Matriculation and Leaving Certificate examinations, the majority of the students gravitated towards a wide range of professions.

I did eventually go to St. Eunan's; and looking back on the years I spent there, I am sure that the school did the best it could with a limited budget and a limited staff, but there were some deficiencies that I do regret. There was hardly any communication between students and staff. This may have been the result of an overworked staff, or the fear of the suspicion of favouritism.

Nevertheless, I often think what a vast help it would have been to us if we had had this rapport. But it was not to be, because in my schooldays we were just emerging from an authoritarian age.

We Irish have the reputation of being great talkers, but it has never been fully appreciated how inarticulate the average rural adolescent can be. It seems a terrible legacy of a rigid authoritarian education system that some of the most important personal resources needed by every human individual were determinedly squashed — most importantly that ability to articulate needs, feelings, and ideas.

For the next fifty years I came across in Irish rural communities the problems that emanate from the demolition of individual self-confidence. How often since, after a meeting, have I been approached by one or two individuals who would make some worthwhile points to me, and when I would say "Why didn't you stand up at the meeting and voice these points?" the answer invariably would be "Ah, well, you see, I was too shy".

Towards the end of my schooldays my mind was torn between two careers. I admit unashamedly that the two had one thing in common, the helping of as wide a range of people as possible, and in the process helping my country which had suffered so much. I was attracted to medicine, and I was also attracted to the priesthood. There were some aspects of a doctor's work, however, which repelled me such as the repulsive nature of some diseases and the awesome responsibility of assisting at childbirth.

At the same time, as a healthy adolescent, I was attracted by girls. If I opted for the priesthood I would be required to renounce marriage. I pondered this for quite some time, but I was immensely swayed by the transience of sexual attraction. What, I asked myself, would happen if she got bored with me or I with her? Life could be very difficult unless there was a completely permanent union of hearts and minds.

But the priesthood offered me a permanent love of people and a love of the work I would be required to do for them. It combined the spiritual, where the results could be inestimable, and the mundane, where in the context of fifty or sixty years ago, the only social worker I could see was the priest. But the real clincher in my deliberations was my absolute conviction in the existence of God and my complete belief in the teachings of Christ.

It was Christ who said, "Do not lay up for yourselves treasures on earth, where rust and moth consume, and where

27

thieves break in and steal: but lay up for yourselves treasures in Heaven."

And again: "I was hungry and you gave Me to eat . . . . in so far as you did this to one of the least of these brothers of mine you did it to Me."

And again: "Whoever exalts himself shall be humbled and whoever humbles himself shall be exalted."

The two aspects of this teaching which most appealed to me were the futility and danger of greed for the accumulation of earthly goods, and the necessity of doing good to the needy of the world. I am quite sure that the first of these has coloured my life since, and developed within me an abhorrence of anything that smacks of rapacity or greed. My mind was made up, and I decided to study for the priesthood.

So, the next step in my education after Matriculation was St. Patrick's College, Maynooth, where I arrived in September 1930 at the age of twenty. What first impressed me about Maynooth were its long history and traditions, and also its origins. Founded at the end of the eighteenth century when the Penal Laws were still in force, the college was the result of a policy decision by the British government of the time, which was not dictated by any love of the Catholic Irish. The decision to fund the college was a matter of expediency because despite the Penal Laws which outlawed the priests in Ireland, young men were smuggled from Ireland to the Continent to be educated and ordained as priests. The British feared that these young men would absorb radical ideas on the Continent which would be uncomfortable for their own establishment in Ireland. Hence, for policy sake, the British government encouraged the foundation of a national seminary at Maynooth.

When I happened to examine the table-ware in the college, I noticed it was embossed with the legend "St. Patrick's R.C.C." This I assumed to be "St. Patrick's Roman Catholic College", but was quickly informed that the "R.C.C." meant Royal Catholic College. Naturally, this offended all my republican principles.

Such are the vagaries of history, and I often considered

that the British government of those far-off days might have had other thoughts if they had realised what a hot-bed of nationalism they were actually creating in Maynooth.

True, there did emerge from Maynooth many bishops and priests who were very conservative, but numbers of Irish clerics were leaders in the preservation of our culture, traditions, and identity, and were fearless spokesmen against our country's many injustices and woes.

As one passes along the corridors of Maynooth, one will see scores of portraits of these past giants who etched their names on Irish history and of them all perhaps the most striking is the portrait of Archbishop MacHale, the "Lion of the West", where the artist captures the granite-like face which had become seamed with scars from the worries of many a steadfast stance against British policy in Ireland. His fearless advocacy of the rights of the people of the West and his constant defence of the use of the Irish language carved for him a place in history.

I am quite sure that the courage of many of these men who spoke out bravely on behalf of their people imbued us all with a spirit of national commitment and the tradition of their courage continues to forge strong links between the priests and people of Ireland today.

Discipline in the Maynooth of my time was exceedingly strict; but it didn't particularly irritate the students. Time and again we were admonished to leave the college if we felt the discipline too harsh. Indeed, I vaguely felt at the time that it was a good thing, because it posed a challenge to the idealism of young students on the brink of manhood. But there was one danger about it.

Individualism of any kind was frowned upon, and often extirpated, with the evident danger of moulding us all in a uniform shape and denying initiative of any kind. I believe my later, rather extrovert nature was a rebellion against those Maynooth days. Rigidity was even carried into our performance of amateur drama, and I remember one or two cases where a student was called to task by authority for being too flamboyant in his role on the stage. It is quite possible that this attempt at standardisation had a con-

29

siderable effect on many young priests after they took up their duties.

The first three years in Maynooth were the university years, in which we studied logic and the several branches of philosophy, physiology and elocution. In addition to this, each of us was required to take one of the normal university subjects for a degree.

The remaining four years were years of specialised study for the priesthood in the various branches of theology and scripture, as well as canon law and liturgy. But the Maynooth experience was, most of all, an exercise in meditation, prayer, and discipline.

However, it is with the college playing fields, the private discussions and public debates, the college dramatic society, and the college choir that my fondest memories linger, for it was here that there were forged deep personal friendships which had never been attained before, and could never be attained afterwards. And it was here that one really came to appreciate the true value of a cross-section of young Irishmen who were well educated and charged with idealism.

My idea of the priesthood may have differed from the popular image — that he was a man who lived a blameless life and that he was a mediator between God and man, both by example and ministration. This popular estimate, though correct, and indeed essential, was much too limited for me. Human beings are composed of body and soul, and in working for people I knew that there could be no dichotomy: I could not always isolate the soul and leave physical, social and economic needs to be attended to by somebody else. Consequently, I felt that the priest must become interested in the material and social needs of people as well.

Of course, I realised that there are many such needs in the community that a priest would have neither the time nor the competence to deal with. Nevertheless, there are vast areas in justice and charity which are often by-passed by humanity, and there are uncounted millions who are suffering from this indifference. My whole being demanded that principles of justice and charity be translated into action, and that if other people would not do so, I would attempt to lead the way.

How little did I realise that this attitude would earn me more criticism than acclaim. For down the years I have fought a running battle with bureaucrats and theorists who were never involved at field level. These were people who would stand idly by, secure in their own little jobs and allow decay and neglect to find its own level, and who were ever ready to strike with "I told you so", if I made a mistake. But I have always been sustained by the motto of the late Canon Hayes which was — "Better to light one candle than forever curse the darkness". My motto was more radical — "Better to light ten candles even though nine of them are extinguished."

Etched forever on my memory will be the splendid grandeur of ordination day. The pealing organ, the ethereal polyphony of the college choir; the crowded college chapel; all blended into an atmosphere which was highly dramatic and yet perennial. And then came the long procession of candidates. All Ireland was represented there — they came from Wexford to Donegal and from Antrim to Kerry, from villages, countryside, and towns. Their gait was solemn but their minds were joyous. Tears of joy and sadness were shed by relatives as they watched transfixed — for this was the parting of the ways. These young men were to remain in the world, but they were not to be of it.

The procession of *ordinandi* moved steadily towards the high altar and the ordaining prelate. They wore neither epaulette, nor sword, nor scabbard, and yet they were to be commissioned as officers. They wore the long white garments which were their insignia of innocence, purity, and peace. On arrival they gave no smart salute. Instead, as they wheeled to their allotted places, they prostrated themselves to give their vows. For these, although they were to become officers, were to become servants of all, and their chivalry was to be the chivalry of God.

But as we walked through the ancient gates of Maynooth College a few days later, a shade of sadness seemed to envelop us all. Goodbyes were said, but with some of us we knew it would be a last farewell. For many of us were going overseas. Some would never return, whilst others would be

31

scattered throughout the length and breadth of Ireland, and would rarely meet, if at all. As for myself, I had arranged to go on loan to the diocese of Southwark which comprised South London, Surrey and Sussex, and the speedy trans-ference from the cloisters of Maynooth to the streets of London was a change indeed.

CHAPTER IV

I rounded the corner on my way to a sick call in the hospital and came face to face with a middle-aged man hurrying in my direction. I wished him a cheery good morning. He transfixed me with an icy stare at ten paces, and hurried on. I had forgotten that I was not at home in Ireland. I was in another country, and I was in London.

My first impression of English people was that they were distinctly cold and formal. It took some time to realise that this was an urban population which was completely different from a rural population where everybody knew everybody else; and being city-folk, they had an inbred wariness of cultivating acquaintanceships or friendships on the first, or even the second meeting.

I think it is generally assumed that country people are at a loss in a great city — that they make many blunders and are prone to stare wide-mouthed at their unusual surroundings. This may well be true, but I'm sure it is equally true that the urban dweller finds it awkward to adjust to rural surroundings.

Urbanity does not necessarily mean slickness, and rusticity does not necessarily mean slowness. However, the lines of division are not so sharply drawn nowadays as they were when I set foot in London forty years ago, because in those days young people did not roam the cities and countries as they do today.

I never had a holiday before I was ordained a priest for the simple reason that there was no spare money, and there was much work to be done during holiday-time on the farm at home. All my upbringing being in the country, I had dreaded the thought of being assigned to a city, but there was little choice, and in London I found myself beginning my work as a priest in strange surroundings and among a strange people. True, they talked the same language, albeit with a different accent, and a different turn of phrase, but their thought processes and their outlook were very different indeed.

There was no question of my settling down without work for a few days. My work was waiting for me literally from the hour I arrived. This was probably a good thing because it gave me little time in which to feel sorry for myself. Nevertheless, I can distinctly recall the first Sunday evening in London when all the work was done, and I suddenly realised that I had nowhere to go and nobody to visit. In all that vast city, there was not a single person whom I could really call an acquaintance much less a friend. I remember going out and walking around one of those "commons" which make London distinctive among cities, and feeling very much alone as I walked.

In Wandsworth, close by Clapham Junction, I lived in the parish priest's house, where his mother was our housekeeper. He was a lively character: Irish born and English educated, he was an interesting mixture.

Particular work I recall from those early years in Wandsworth was the setting up of a youth club where I placed much of the emphasis on amateur dramatics. But the everyday duties predominated, for the work of a priest in an English parish was much more demanding than in an Irish parish. Weekly calls were expected by many, and in a city parish hospital calls were very important. But the experience was both demanding and rewarding, and I was to carry a lesson with me on my return to Ireland about the importance of a priest getting to know people, and they him.

As the weeks and the years followed, I certainly changed my opinion of the English. This, I discovered, was a friendly people. They were not prepared to trust you the first or even the second time, but given enough time and opportunity they could cultivate a friendship which ran very deep. During those years that I spent with this trustful and truly friendly people, I often wondered why it was that our country and theirs had been locked in strife for so many hundreds of years, and how it was that in their name were perpetrated so many injustices and wrongs upon our race.

For all the stark materialism which surrounded them, they were an innocent people and they often enjoyed my own brand of Irish humour which specialised in defusing particularly formal occasions or conventions into occasions of mirth. I remember meeting some of the upper middle class who greeted me with a languid "How do you do". I took a puckish delight in replying "Fine thanks, how are you yourself?" As this posed another question they seemed completely nonplussed. Nevertheless they loved the Irish for their humour. But they were often wary of engaging in an argument with an Irish person, because they somehow felt that he was barometric and would very quickly lose his temper. Such an embarrassing situation, according to their code, must be avoided at all costs.

The English had another quality which, after my first year in England was amply demonstrated. This was their tenacity and courage. Hitler marched into Poland in September 1939, and the Second World War began. After the débacle of Dunkirk, all hell broke loose over the London skies, and as I went about my duties, comforting the homeless and the maimed and attending to the dying, I encountered everywhere stoical courage, coloured here and there with what struck me as a sub-human hatred of the perpetrators. For, as I have often discovered since, the English have a special brand of dislike for those who oppose them.

In the autumn and winter after Dunkirk, the German air raids on the military aerodromes and the suburbs and the city of London became very serious. At first the air battles were fought in daylight but gradually the pattern changed to regular nightly bombings. It brought home to me the sadness and the cruelty of modern warfare, where the civilian suffers most. Several people in the parish simply could not endure the sleeplessness and the tension, and decided to go elsewhere. One could never relax. Standing talking to a friend at my front door during a daylight air-raid we suddenly heard a

35

thud. It was the brass cap of a shell which embedded itself in the ground a few feet away.

Like many other people who were required to be on duty during air-raids, I was equipped with a steel helmet but I'm afraid that I was not London's best air-raid warden. Hearing the clatter of a stick of incendiary bombs on our roof one night I charged to my first bomb armed with a crockery basin with which I tried to smother the bomb. Before my eyes the basin melted in the intense heat. However I learned my lesson: sand or clay was the answer.

Of course, the grim air blitz had its humorous side betimes. An Irish priest lived in the next parish in Wandsworth. His house was quite close to the headquarters of the London South West fire brigade. He often visited me and we compared notes on the havoc of the night before. I constantly maintained, bravely, that I was really in the front line, being close to Clapham Junction which was a prime target. But he contended that his situation was much worse. At length he called on me one day and he seemed to show relief. "Gosh Mac", said he "they got the fire brigade headquarters last night, but the problem is this — do they know that they have got it?"

One evening I dropped in to visit Dr. and Mrs. Kirwan, an Irish couple whose company I came to cherish, when an air raid was at its height over our area. Mrs. Kirwan made the tea but the noise of falling bombs got closer and closer. At length the scream of "our bomb" coming through the air became so loud that we knew that this was "it". "Into the hallway!" shouted the doctor, "it is between two inside walls." We jumped: the bomb fell: the house danced on its foundations and with falling ceiling we could scarcely see each other. Mrs. Kirwan turned a deathly white and I saw the doctor make the sign of the cross. I immediately preened myself on being the most unflappable and began to make some wisecrack, but my teeth let me down. I could not keep them from chattering and no coherent words came forth.

I was fortunate to be spared many of the gruesome tasks of attending to the mutilated and the dead who were quickly moved to hospitals far from me. But my most difficult task lay in trying to console the bereaved whether death had struck in London or on the battle-front. And they were many. One mother in our parish had four sons called into the army, and only one returned.

My saddest casualty of all was a young girl of nine years who, as a result of an air-raid, had to have her leg amputated. I visited her on the following day and to my surprise I found her in quite good spirits. The nurses and patients had convinced her that her leg would grow again. Whenever I think of modern war I think of that girl.

But though the ordinary people suffered in the English cities, my thoughts went out, too, to the German city dwellers who endured what must have been a much more massive onslaught from the air in what was euphemistically termed "blanket bombing" or "pattern bombing".

The *casus belli* was noble and necessary, but how much more noble it would have been if all the allies had relinquished their claims and their "spheres of influence" over subjected territories. East Poland, Estonia, Latvia, Lithuania and other proud independent nations have disappeared into the insatiable maw of Russian imperialism, whilst it was left to India, Vietnam and several African peoples to fight their own wars for self-determination and there still remain pockets of imperialism which, through subjection or manipulation, have not won the dignity of freedom yet.

I yearn now for a world war of a very different kind. Not the projected nuclear war, but a war against the claims of nations to territories which are not their own. It is a war which should be fought against those who have knowingly and barbarously induced poverty, humiliation, and degradation in countries of the third world. If there is a spark of civilisation beneath the veneer, this is the world war which should be promptly fought, and fought with all the billions that are now being squandered on instruments of destruction.

* * *

After four-and-a-half years in Wandsworth I was transferred to St. Mary Cray, near Orpington in Kent. I arrived only a few weeks after the church, school and priest's house

37

had been wiped out by a German landmine; and every minute of my spare time was taken up with collecting money. My main means of doing this was running football pools, and nearly every week I would take the train to London to go collecting there. I remained in Kent for a further four-and-a-half years until I was transferred to Brighton, by the sea in Sussex, where three curates shared the parish priest's house.

My work during those ten years in England was not confined to English people. Scattered throughout the industrial centres were many young Irish men and women. The Irish had been migrating to England ever since the Great Famine in Ireland in 1847, and in the immediate post-war period, attracted by the vast opportunities in the building trade particularly, they came over in droves.

In the early days of immigration from Ireland in the second half of the nineteenth century, the Irish immigrant certainly made a bad impression. He was immensely poor; he was lonely; he was ill-fed, and in his leisure hours he sought an escape from his boarding-house and solace from his loneliness in resort to the public house. The result was that there grew up in England an impression that all Irish were dissolute and quarrelling drunkards. This impression was excusable, but unfortunately the depth of poverty and deprivation to which English misrule had degraded the average Irishman was never considered. But during my sojourn in England, the immigrant who came over from the Republic was a different type. He was poor, but unlike his predecessor of the nineteenth century, he was not undernourished, destitute, or uneducated.

Nevertheless, it was a matter of no small irritation to observe the downright antagonism of a large section of the British press to the Irish and to Ireland, which seems to linger on to a lesser extent to this day. Even a unit of the English Catholic press seemed to adopt the same trend in a pathetic attempt to distance English Catholicism from Irish Catholicism. In my ten years in England I rarely ever read anything in the popular press that was not derogatory to Ireland or the Irish. And I have consistently asked myself the question ever since: Why do they hate us so much?

The Irish emigrant came from a land which had asserted her right to independence by resort to armed revolt in every century during the seven centuries of British domination, and when eventually the 1916-22 War of Independence succeeded in attaining independence for twenty-six out of the thirty-two counties, it had left a country of slightly over three million people — almost entirely agricultural — with no capital and neither industry nor the tradition of industry. It was on this sparse economic base that the new Irish governments had to build. Practically every country in Europe had a head-start on the new Irish state in industrial development, by about a hundred years. The area where there had been development in industry in Ireland, the North-East, was now partitioned off from independent Ireland and was attached to the British crown.

The family of the peasant farmer was no longer content to derive a pittance from the family income and with standards of living rising all around him and no large industrial base at home to absorb him, what was more natural than that he should fly to the large labour market on his doorstep and migrate to England.

This may have been acceptable to the expanding British economy; it may have benefited the Irish worker, but it certainly did not benefit the country he had left, and in some cases it was disastrous for the young person from Ireland who was transplanted from a country home and parental guidance to the strange and sometimes dangerous surroundings of urban life.

As I met, and sometimes helped, many of these Irish immigrants, the idea kept growing in my mind that this was all wrong. Here was a vast body of Irish youth flocking into England. In nine cases out of ten they were excellent people of whom any country could be justly proud, and Ireland could ill afford to lose them. Moreover, I thought that it ill-befitted our dignity as a nation in the first few decades of independence to have to depend on that very nation from which we had wrested our freedom to help to absorb our youth.

It is true that the Irish people came in search of work, but it is also true that after finding that work they helped to build a stronger Britain. It is true that the British welcomed this invasion of first class labour to man their building sites and many of their social services, but it is also true that in many cases the intrusion of the Irish was resented and individual Irish people were cold-shouldered.

All these considerations kept prickling in my mind and I gradually resolved that when I returned to Ireland I would sound a note of alarm about emigration, and even more, I would do what I could to arrest it in whatever parish or district to which I was assigned.

The time came when I was recalled to my native Donegal. Though I was very glad to go home, nevertheless it was with a heavy heart that I left England. I had become so involved in one project after another and had come to respect the sincerity of the people. I had been with them in their war, I had been with them in peace. I had worked in London, in Kent, and in Brighton, and now I bade goodbye to Sussex by the sea to go to another sea — a wilder sea — for my first assignment in Ireland was on the gale-swept island of Tory, nine miles off the North-West coast of Donegal, where I arrived in a small boat in June of 1947.

CHAPTER V

It is surprising to find the number of people who have a nostalgic feeling about islands. In their minds they invest them with a certain mystique. I suppose this is natural enough for people who are gripped by the "get away from it all" mentality. But it must be admitted that very few of these people have spent a few years on a lonely, isolated, island. The measure of my frustration can be judged by the precision with which I counted the length of my sojourn on Tory Island. It was four years, six months, and twelve days. In my case, the adjustment must have been particularly arduous because I was in the prime of manhood; I had left the swirling life of the city in which I had been engaged in many projects. On an island I could find very few people who were willing to have a good discussion on international affairs or current events.

The islanders were extremely friendly, and even too courteous. Consequently I found life very lonely. Indeed, I approached my bishop to get his permission to return to England permanently but his answer was a blank "No". So strongly did I feel about this that I sought and got an appointment with the Papal Nuncio. But this was not to be, because on my way to the appointment I picked up the morning paper only to discover that the Papal Nuncio had died in his sleep the previous night.

As islands go, Tory was comparatively small, being three miles long and about half a mile wide. There were almost forty houses and about two hundred and seventy people on the island. I lived in the priest's house, and my house-keeper was able to help me find my feet with all her information about the local people. The pattern of emigration was casual: very few migrated permanently, but many departed in the spring to work in Scotland, returning in the autumn, and many went into temporary domestic service in the Six Counties.

I began to improve the social life by establishing a drama club. On the nights when we produced a play the scene was hilarious. Our theatre was makeshift: our stage was composed of planks placed over barrels; our lighting was the Tilley lamp. The building would be packed. Indeed, all the islanders who could walk would be present. Audience control presented a difficulty especially when the curtain went up. This stemmed principally from the noisy speculation as to the identity of the actors and actresses. I remember one occasion when a stolid fisherman who was a little deaf placed himself in a strategic position right beside the footlights so that he would miss nothing. The curtain went up and the noise and laughter from the audience was so great and so prolonged that he felt he was missing the dialogue on the stage, and in sheer frustration he jumped to his feet, faced the audience and, shaking his fist, shouted *"Bígidh in bhur dtost!"*, which, gently translated, means "Keep quiet!"

Mainland residents might be tempted to be patronising or even supercilious to islanders. This would be a gross mistake, for the average islander was quite well educated and in his or her traditional battle with the sea and the elements had acquired a sharpness of intellect and perception far above the average on the mainland where life was easier. Isolation had made them practically self-sufficient, and in this battle their minds and their deftness were honed to a remarkable degree.

In an effort to prevent migration and to introduce more spending money I tried to found a knitting industry on the island. I wrote to, and I visited several government departments in Dublin in a vain effort to persuade some government agency to initiate a small industry there. I was convinced that the islanders with their natural dexterity would be very easily trained. But it was not to be. My proposals were received with courtesy, but the prolonged negotiations amounted to nothing and I was eventually advised by one department to use my powers of persuasion in having the islanders transferred to homes on the mainland. This might have made economic sense but culturally it would have been a disaster. The Irish language was the natural medium on Tory. It would have been dissipated and lost if there had been a diaspora. This was my first encounter with government departments. There were to be many more.

I tried to create work for myself. I promptly ran up a debt by doing necessary improvements to the church. This created a chain reaction for I had to eliminate the debt by organising social functions like dances, concerts, dramas, whist drives, and bazaars. Some of these had to be organised from the bottom up because the islanders had no previous experience of them. It was all great fun, and certainly one could not wish for more adaptable pupils.

In my anxiety to be active I even went out to the fields to help with the harvest. The people must have thought I was mad because they had some queer idea that priests should not do manual work. I remember on one occasion going to the help of a farmer whose only child — a daughter — was attempting to build a cart load of corn on a very windy day. All the neighbours were busy with their own crops. I thought it a shame that a young girl should be required to do such a heavy task, for the farmer had no son. So I volunteered to build the load in her stead. But it seemed that the old cart was not intended to hold such a massive weight as mine, especially with the wind buffeting me hither and thither as I built the load. Fancy my astonishment when I felt the whole cart sagging underneath. Suddenly the farmer yelled that the shaft had broken. I slid down to *terra firma* and was quick to offer my services to run for help. But I made sure not to meet the farmer until a few days had passed.

The island was replete with ancient monuments and legend and lore. High on the list of legends was that of Balor of the Evil Eye who is represented in folklore as a king and is said to have established a fortress on Tory, the site of which is pointed out to this day. Nearby are the remains of many circular "beehive" dwellings. Balor could not have been a very social chap because he seemed to have spent most of his life in wars of plunder on the mainland, but he was evidently sagacious enough to have made the isolated island his impregnable retreat.

So rich is the island in lore and legend that hardly a rock or promentary does not bear a Gaelic name and in true Gaelic style each of these names is descriptive of some event, some personage or some geophysical peculiarity.

A local story tells of six brothers and one sister who arrived on the island in the early centuries of Christianity. They seemed very pious but were so emaciated by their long sea journey that they soon died, and to this day the clay from their grave is considered to have great powers. Tory Island boasts a round tower, which served as a refuge when sea pirates descended on the island. St. Colmcille, the great Donegal saint, brought Christianity to the island and many are the stories that are handed down about his confrontation with the pagans of Tory. When leaving, he bequeathed to the islanders a *turas* or pilgrimage to ensure the continuity of penance and prayer. At a later stage a former pagan artifact called "The Cursing Stone" became intertwined with the ritual of the *turas*; but it was forbidden by the priest and its whereabouts are now unknown.

Although the island life had many compensations — no telephone, infrequent mail, and the complete absence of callers at awkward hours, I still wanted to move. I was young and energetic, and I fretted and felt frustrated that some of the best years of my life were being frittered away when there was so much work to be done elsewhere. I could walk from one end of the island to the other in an hour. I used to sit on the little sandy beach and contemplate. I even sang to the incoming and inquisitive seals who would draw nearer and nearer to investigate the origin of this peculiar sound, and I resolved that whenever my transfer came I would release such a burst of energy that others would be amazed.

My pastoral work was easy, for if I wished, I could easily visit each family once a week. The islanders all spoke the Irish language and though my appointment to the island was

44

precisely because I was supposed to be a good Gaelic speaker, this was a mistake, because I only had book knowledge of Irish and I found a great language barrier between them and myself. However, it was not an insurmountable barrier and a compromise in communications was very quickly worked out.

One great difficulty I did find. I was most anxious to become more proficient in speaking Irish, but to do so one must listen, and listen carefully and often, as others speak. This I found to be impossible for such was the courtesy extended by the islanders to the priest that they found it intolerable and completely lacking in good manners to carry on a conversation whilst the priest sat dumbly by.

The only link with the outside world was by radio telephone and mail boat. The latter was supposed to ply to the mainland, which was nine miles away, three times each week, but of course there were times during the winter when several weeks passed without any physical link with the outside world at all. If the period of isolation was considerably extended, the food stocks on the island began to run low. The island was very damp because of the all-pervading salt-water spray, which in times of severe storm completely blanketed it. Consequently, stocks of most kinds of food began to perish after about three weeks. Salt, butter, flour and cigarettes were the first to become unusable, and life could be very unpleasant indeed.

But in these times of hardship the islanders showed their greatest kindness and self-sacrifice. They evidently considered that the priest, being a mainlander, was a tenderfoot and was not geared to withstand these hardships. They would try therefore to cushion him by bringing chickens and eggs and any worthwhile delicacy they could think of. Such gestures were embarrassing in the extreme but they served to cement my friendship with this lonely people.

Such was the love of the islanders for their way of life that, even when they emigrated for a period, they almost always returned to spend six months of each year at home. The acquisition of money was not an overriding factor in their lives. It was amusing to see them return — especially the girls — after a period of some months working elsewhere.

45

They would return with the very latest fashions prevailing and had a particular addiction to the brightest colours. I suppose this penchant for bright colours was in some way a reaction to the comparatively drab and overall grey environment in which they lived.

But my days on the island of Tory were numbered, and the telegram came in December 1951 which transferred me to another remote part of County Donegal, but this time I was to be on the mainland. I remember the morning I stood on the boat and gave my blessing to the islanders for the last time. Their faces seemed sad and my heart was heavy as I bade farewell to this innocent people so unspoiled by the world. Their life was a hard one but it was far from the rush and bustle and many of the cares that beset people living in the ordinary world of busy roads and cities, and as the years unfolded I had time to envy them their uncomplicated existence.

The great Donegal saint of the seventh century — St. Colmcille — took upon himself the evangelising of the pockets of paganism which still existed in the remoter parts of his native county. At a later period he set out for Iona where he established a famous monastery. Tory Island is one of the places in Donegal with which his name is intimately linked, and it seemed to be my fate to retrace his footsteps for the place to which I was now assigned not only was evangelised by him, but actually bore his name. It was called Glencolumbkille.

CHAPTER VI

A mighty battle must have been fought over the ages between Europe and the turbulent Atlantic. Ireland, by its geographical position was in the vanguard of that battle. However, a compromise was reached because from Donegal to Kerry the towering cliffs stand guard and here and there the ocean in its more subdued moods is permitted to penetrate a hundred sheltered inlets and gently kiss the silver strands. Glencolumbkille is one of the places where this battle must have raged most fiercely.

The parish of Glencolumbkille — some one hundred and fifty square miles of it — begins with the village of Carrick, nestling at the foot of Sliabh Liag and overlooking Teelin harbour and salmon-fishing estuary. The huge mass of Sliabh Liag dominates the landscape, for it stands like a mighty fortress and glowers at the Atlantic beneath in perpetual defiance.

Five miles further west, the road overlooks the beautiful glen of Columbkille. It is no exaggeration to say that it is among Ireland's most beautiful valleys; and it is certainly one of the most secluded. The scenery is breath-taking, whether it is the glen itself ringed on three sides by mountains, and opening onto a sandy beach and the sea, or the houses of the glen as they clutch precariously to its hillsides.

One can sit here and allow the imagination to run back over the centuries until one sees the first settlers who came here to a green and fertile valley some five thousand years ago and whose burial places remain in evidence. By the time the Celts came the bogs had begun to grow. Here, supposedly,

47

on the banks of the river, the druids raised a magical mist to prevent the advance of St. Colmcille, the founder of Christianity in these parts. He parted the mist as if it were the Red Sea, and the beautifully incised cross-slabs bear testimony to the intense activity of the early Christians. In many later centuries the alarums of conquest, battle and oppression sounded, and famine and emigration came in their wake.

Like so many other places along the Western coast, the glen's beauty is matched only by the poverty of agricultural resources. Before emigration began in earnest, in the early nineteenth century, its economy was becoming poorer because of the continued subdivision of farms among families. Earlier, the policy of the English zealot, Cromwell, may have had an effect on Glencolumbkille. That policy was summed up in his infamous dictum "To hell or to Connaught" for the Irish, and I am sure Glencolumbkille, among other areas, felt some pressure from the displaced Irish from the East. The result was that the area became overcrowded, vastly out of proportion to its natural resources. But then in the early nineteenth century the blood-letting started: emigration began.

It was never intended that Ireland would benefit by the Industrial Revolution which made England so populous and so great. Ireland was to remain an agricultural country which would supply the English with cheap food. By law, the Catholic Irish were denied education until 1829 and that meant a barrier to the services or the professions. Consequently, because of the endemic redundancy in an agricultural economy, there was only one course left to the majority of Irish people and that was emigration.

But worse was to come. What started as a trickle became a flood when the staple diet of the Irish people failed in two successive years, 1847 and 1848. Through starvation and emigration the population of Ireland was halved. So devastating was this famine that the leading English newspaper reported that the Celt would soon become as scarce on the banks of the Shannon as the Red Indian on the shores of Manhattan. From this point on emigration became a way of life among the Irish.

48

When we won independence for the greater part of our country, our native government had no industrial base. Shortly afterwards came the "hungry 'thirties" and then the Second World War. While many of the economic problems of the new state were inherited ones, and Ireland remained in many ways dependent, our own native governments were not blameless. Much is contained in a reported exchange between Peadar O'Donnell, the writer and radical from Donegal, and Eamonn de Valera. "If you had been in power instead of me," said Dev, "there still would have been a million emigrants." "Ah, yes," replied Peadar, "but they would have been a different million!" It was not until the early 'sixties that our government attempted to establish an industrial base to staunch the flow of emigration.

I was conscious of all the debilitating effects of our emigration when I arrived in Glencolumbkille as curate. I had met the flower of our youth as emigrants in England and I knew that no country could ever cherish its citizens if it was unable to support them with employment. And here I saw it happening before my eyes, for Glencolumbkille was dying — and the killer disease was emigration. There was no industry apart from intermittent weaving; there was no hope of prosperity for those who worked the land. The vitality of the community was ebbing fast. When I settled in as curate at the beginning of 1952 and for several years afterwards, the marriage rate hardly ever exceeded four or five marriages per annum. It was easy to see that no community could retain its numerical strength at this rate. On reaching the age of sixteen or seventeen, about eighty percent of the boys and girls were emigrating and indeed in a few cases, where the parents were young, the home was abandoned and the whole family emigrated. The population was resolving itself into the old and the very young, and it was clear that before long we would only have the old.

A fierce resolve gripped my mind. Perhaps I was influenced by the doughty cliffs that surrounded me. Perhaps I was influenced by the traditional nationalism in which I was nurtured. But certainly I am sure that I was moved by the injustice that had been done to our people over the centuries.

The tears of parting that I witnessed in my youth, and which I now witnessed in Glencolumbkille, activated and solidified the determination in my heart. I was not so naive that I thought I could put at right the wrongs of a nation, but I felt that I could add a little bit of stimulus to self-help which could arouse other isolated communities across the land.

I expected our governments to fulfil their responsibility to support and often create job opportunities for our people, but I was realist enough to know that we were at the end of the queue and that by the time help came it would be too late unless we first raised the standard of revolt ourselves. As a priest, my main duty was to the spiritual needs of the people. But as a priest I must be committed to justice and charity, and if there was nobody else on the ground to implement them I would attempt to do so even if I altered the traditional image of the priest, and dabbled in the mundane. Writing now, thirty years later, I am glad to assert that amidst successes and failures, I have not changed this outlook one iota.

Rural communities are different from urban communities. In the urban setting there is usually the ebb and flow of a changing population and the consequent interaction of new ideas. Rural communities generally can expect no such replacements, and the exodus from them usually siphons off the more entrepreneurial and ambitious types. This process carried on for over a hundred years is bound to leave behind it a debilitated population where neglect has given way to despair, and despair to introversion, apathy and conservatism. This does not mean that there was nobody left in Glencolumbkille who was anxious to change. By no means. Certainly more than one-third of the population would follow a lead if it were given, but several of these doubted if a lead could be given from within whilst most of the community were so divided in their allegiance to the two principal political parties that they felt there would be a reproach to their party if there was independent community action.

I have often been criticised for taking this stand, and indeed one very prominent politician advised me to leave things as they were and that eventually these scattered communities of

Western Ireland would find their own level of decay.

There have been some who in an effort to belittle our stand in Glencolumbkille have said that all the things we did there would have been done eventually by government. I doubt that. Judging by my own experience over the first few years when I did the rounds of government departments there was no help forthcoming, and if and when it eventually came, it would have been too late because a rural community can reach the point of no return. A pioneer in any endeavour ploughs a lonely furrow. I felt that in the ensuing years I was constantly trying to charge other people's batteries whereas there was nobody to charge my own. The muted voices of critics in high places engendered within me a stubbornness but the love of country, and the love of God, sustained me.

CHAPTER VII

In order to launch any community project, one must have a representative base, and the base in Glencolumbkille was an elected parish council of some of the more concerned citizens.

Elected annually on 1 January — all those over twenty-one were eligible to vote — it had no powers in law; but it had the potential to identify problems and to generate pressure for improved amenities and employment opportunities. Parish or community councils are often criticised as talking shops. But I was lucky, for in the years in which I was associated with them I found a most dedicated, reliable and knowledgeable body of men and women. They were kind enough to invite me to become their chairman. It was a happy marriage.

Looking back on those days from a distance, and at the risk of appearing pretentious, I reckon that I was the type of person needed for I produced many ideas and the council discussed them from the standpoint of local knowledge, and a consensus was attained. The council members tried to sell the ideas in their different neighbourhoods, and I myself went from house to house endeavouring to generate enthusiasm.

Under the impact of this swirl of activity the council's stature and confidence grew, and even though I was prepared to absorb all the criticism if projects were unpopular, or if things went wrong, I found impeccable loyalty.

I well remember one of our first meetings. We had invited representatives of Gaeltarra Éireann to meet us in order to obtain a better deal for the weavers of hand-woven tweed. Gaeltarra Éireann was the state-sponsored body responsible for economic and cultural development in areas where the Irish language still survived. It has since been replaced by Údarás na Gaeltachta, which is charged with the same responsibilities. It would be an exaggeration to say that either body has been eminently successful.

The weavers had been weaving for Gaeltarra Éireann in annexes to their homes, but the supply of yarn for the looms was so intermittent and the conditions of collecting the finished webs so unsatisfactory that most of the weavers were quite dispirited. At the meeting several members of our parish council made eloquent contributions in a constructive manner. I had come to the conclusion that the only way in which the matter could be resolved was by building a factory for the weaving of handwoven tweed. I felt that it was only in this way that the weavers could be guaranteed sufficient work at a fair wage. But much water was to pass under the bridge before this was achieved.

In my contribution to the meeting I listed what I then considered to be the five curses of Glencolumbkille. These were — no industry, no electricity, no public water supply, unsurfaced roads, and no dispensary. I forgot that Willie Cunningham, the local reporter, was present and I was quite shocked to see in front page banner headlines in the next issue of the *Donegal Democrat*, the caption, "The Five Curses of Glencolumbkille, by Fr. McDyer".

The representative committee of people which I had was all important, but it very quickly became apparent that we must have a community centre of our own where we could have meetings and make some money by organised entertainments. This was discussed and agreed, and I was advised about a few likely sites.

I may have many faults but procrastination is not one of them. Within days I bought a site for thirty pounds; a block-making machine was purchased; a few hundred pounds was borrowed from the bank by Jim Doherty, a local grocer, and member of the council, and myself to add to the few hundred we already had, and from this flimsy financial base we

53

commenced.

The community was appraised of the plan and in general there was consent. The expenditure of money was reduced by the use of voluntary labour. Each day there were upwards of thirty labourers, between skilled and unskilled, and all they received was a midday meal.

The first sod was cut on 7 January, 1953, and true to form I set a target for completion twelve weeks from that date. Of course everybody said I was mad, but there was a method in my madness because if the accomplishment of a project depends on voluntary labour, then its execution must be short, snappy, and efficient. Otherwise it becomes a burden, a bore and a drag. Moreover, in a voluntary labour effort, morale will soon sag if it depends solely on encouragement. Encouragement should be active as well as verbal. Consequently, on every possible occasion I donned overalls and worked with the team. The tempo I set was copied.

I remember, on one occasion, we had a narrow escape from serious accident. Two masons working at each end of a scaffold developed an argument. As the argument became more serious they advanced towards the already overloaded centre of the scaffold, each gesticulating with his trowel. Suddenly there was a splintering crash, and masons, scaffold, bricks and mortar fell to the ground. Everyone was amused but it would have been a different story if anyone had been hurt, because we were not insured.

The emphasis on efficiency and speed was paramount. When ten of the targeted twelve weeks had already gone the roofing had not yet been done. There were two weeks to go, and Jim Doherty, my excellent voluntary clerk of works, told me that we could not meet the deadline. "But we must!" I cried. "I have a pageant organised and everything is made ready for the opening ceremony." "Well" said Jim, "it will take four days to finish the roof." "Nonsense" said I, "we will do it in one. Tell me everything that must be done." Jim told me, and we so streamlined the labour on assembly-line technique that the roof was completed by five p.m. in one day.

In the last few days, work went on to the small hours. The ladies moved in and did great work. At two a.m. on the official opening day I produced two bottles of whiskey and a bottle of wine, and the gleam in the eyes of the workers was like sunshine after a storm!

The hall was formally opened exactly twelve weeks after it had been begun. The people were good enough to chair Jim Doherty and myself down the village street to the opening ceremony. It was our Palm Sunday. But there were many days of crosses and disappointments to follow.

The installation of electricity was our next target, but here we ran into fairly determined opposition by the few. These were mainly ageing householders who had no families, and they had successfully blocked the electrification of Glencolumbkille a few years previously. However, it would be difficult to blame them. Their attitude sprang from their traditionally disenfranchised existence and their isolation from involvement in progress. After all, were they not to fear another alien force from outside? They had good reason to suspect such forces, and progress.

We discussed the matter at committee and there was general consent that we should try again but no one was optimistic. However, I was determined that on this occasion we would not be thwarted, because there could be no worth-while progress without electricity.

I asked the Electricity Supply Board to send down one of their best men to address a general meeting. They did better. They sent down Colm Browne who was a native of the district. The meeting in the community hall was packed, which was a good omen. Colm really excelled himself and I was sure I could feel the vibrations of assent from the audience.

After the meeting ended, I called the council together, apportioned the whole district into areas, and asked each member to take a district and do a snap canvass on the following day. The result was that seventy-four percent of the houses agreed to the installation. But now speed was essential because I knew that several waverers could be dissuaded by those who were opposed, and if our percentage dropped appreciably, the ESB would not move in. Our local canvass placed us at the top of the queue but the ESB insisted on an official canvass. The problem was to have this done before too much erosion of enthusiasm took place.

Each Sunday I watched nervously, after Mass, as one of the most eloquent conservatives spread his message of dissent to willing ears. I drove here and there to meet officials and try to have them commence the canvass. On one occasion I met a commercial traveller who I knew golfed with a director of the ESB. To his surprise I bought him a drink, and in the middle of a glass of brandy when he was at his most mellow, I asked him to intervene vigorously on our behalf.

I could see his Adam's apple pop in surprise. I feel sure he did as I requested because, within a week, the official canvass started. Little did the Glencolumbkille people realise how much speedy installation may have depended on a glass of brandy, the pop of an Adam's apple, and a game of golf!

It was good that I had exerted such pressure, because in the six weeks which had intervened the percentage had dropped from seventy-four to sixty-nine percent. Nevertheless, the work commenced and as it did, one more hazard confronted us. The ESB complained to me again and again that their recruitment of local labour was quite inadequate and that the work would thus be so prolonged that it would be jeopardised. Sufficient workers could not be found because so many were afraid they would lose the dole.

This problem was one which would emerge on many occasions, and not just in Glencolumbkille. With earnings from the land so poor (by 1960 the average income per male farmer in County Donegal was two hundred and fourteen pounds per annum) small farmers were entitled to unemployment assistance. When jobs were created, they competed with the dole; but the difference between opening wages and the dole was not great. Temporary jobs meant losing the dole while the job was on, then suffering delay and difficulties in getting back on the register. So the reluctance to apply for work was both understandable and infuriating. I appealed publicly but without result. This fear of losing the dole was not confined to Glencolumbkille: it was a national malaise.

My reaction was sharp. I wrote a trenchant letter to the late Bill Norton who was Minister for Social Welfare in the government of the time. I forget what I wrote, but among other things I threatened that I would go public with the problem. On the following Monday upwards of thirty extra workers were directed by the Labour Exchange to report for work. It was well for me that my action was never known because my popularity would have plummetted.

The work was completed and those who had previously refused to have electricity in their houses agreed to have it installed. I was determined that the people would be made aware that they had taken a great step forward, so I dramatised the official switch-on. I arranged with the ESB to have the light switched on after dark, and all the people were requested to arrange their switches so that every house, and every street light would be simultaneously illuminated.

I organised a single file procession from the top of the village street to the point where the ceremony would take place. Everyone was attired in period costume. First came the bearer of a rush candle (fortunately the night was calm), next the bearer of an ordinary candle, then the hob-lamp, the hurricane lamp, the wick lamp with globe, the Tilley and Aladdin lamps, and finally the electric torch. The main switch was pulled; the whole area was suddenly illuminated and a new era had begun.

The most important advantage was in terms of industry, but it also meant that labour-saving devices could be introduced into homesteads; and the streets of the villages and surrounds were lit, creating quite a new atmosphere. At the entertainment afterwards, our committee got together and as we toasted each other our smiles had their own special brightness.

CHAPTER VIII

Land is the most natural resource that God has given us; it always irritates me to see it neglected and, being the son of a small farmer myself, I have an instinctive love of land. We discussed this subject in all its aspects at our various council meetings, and of course it received the keen attention of all because the members were farmers or had spent their childhood on their parents' farms. But the problems confronting us in any attempt at improvement were considerable.

First of all, the land was bad, and secondly the average holding was about eight acres. Of these, generally only about one or two acres were arable in each farm; and the people had no money for investment in improvement. Moreover, many farms were in the hands of middle-aged people whose children had emigrated, and a considerable number of them did not like to risk losing the dole by becoming too progressive in farming. These were some of the problems that baffled us as we explored new initiatives.

It was about this time, 1955, that the successor of the one-time landlord in Carrick — six miles from Glencolumbkille village — made it clear that if the people could collect four thousand pounds he would transfer the ownership of the estate to the community. It was an exceedingly generous offer, even by the standards of the nineteen-fifties. My help was enlisted by Enda Cunningham, a local teacher, and together we were consumed with enthusiasm at the prospect, for the estate had a farm of sixty acres, three houses, six lakes, two rivers, and two fishing inlets. My plans for the development of the estate were fairly grandiose, but they were practical. First we would attempt to convert the sixty acres of the estate into a model sheep farm which would be owned by the shareholders in the community. In this I was greatly influenced by the work I had seen done by the Agricultural Institute in Glenamoy, County Mayo. Hopefully this farm would act as a pace-setter for the local sheep-farmers both in the improvement of bad land and in the up-grading of sheep breeding.

Secondly, we would try to involve the people of Teelin, who had been neglected for so long, in the ownership and development of their very fine estuary and bay. The people of Teelin have traditionally been fine fishermen and with the stimulus of ownership they could be encouraged to preserve salmon stocks. I even had a vague idea that salmon could be farmed in the outer reaches of the bay, though in those years of the early 'fifties I had only a faint notion of how this could be done. But I did know that all kinds of crustacean farming could be attempted from oysters down, and I had supreme confidence in the ability of the Teelin fishermen. I always maintained that the time was coming when wild fish would become so scarce that people would be forced into mariculture and aquaculture just as their ancestors eight thousand years ago were forced to abandon the hunting of wild animals and concentrate on agriculture instead. There were six lakes in the estate and it was my intention that these should be developed to their fullest capacity either as attractions for anglers or as fish farms.

Finally there was the old landlord's house with its sur-rounding three or four acres commanding a beautiful view of Teelin Bay. It was the idea of Enda Cunningham, and I shared it with him, that this should contain a restaurant and a holiday-cottage complex. Of all our plans, this was probably the easiest to activate.

These were our dreams and Enda Cunningham and I trudged through the parish enlisting promises of cash here and there, and the people were as generous as their limited resources allowed. But by the time about two thousand pounds had been pledged, two prominent local people began working against us, and they convinced a large section of the

people that it would be better if Gael-Linn made this pur-
chase and that Gael-Linn would give lots of employment. As
the opinion of the community swung towards Gael-Linn our
sources of money dried up. I could have wept with anguish.
It seemed now, as so often, that the credibility of the stranger
superseded that of the locals.

Enda Cunningham and I visited Donall Ó Móráin in Dublin
and offered to co-operate with Gael-Linn, but the reply was a
courteous refusal. Gael-Linn bought the estate and unfortunately their efforts did not prove successful. They seem to
have concentrated mainly on farming pigs and sheep, but
much more input of capital would have been required to
realise the full potential. Indeed, in the light of my subsequent frustration in trying to sell new ideas to state bodies
to obtain grants, I feel that we would probably have encountered similar difficulties.

This was the time when I sprung one of my wild schemes
on the council which, like so many others, was still-born. I
was fortunate to have in the district an agricultural adviser
of the very highest calibre named Michael Burke. Between us
we had a splendid working relationship. Usually I produced
the germ of an idea and Michael would hone it and refine it
until it became quite credible.

The central farm unit was one such idea. It was intended
to provide a strong stimulus to agriculture and was divided
into three phases. First there was to be an acre under glass,
heated by local fuel, which would produce three crops per
year: onions, tomatoes and chrysanthemums. This would be
operated by women because women formed the greatest percentage of our emigrants, and moreover, I had seen the girls
working in the Land Army in Britain during the war and they
were superior to men. They were more conscientious and
gave greater attention to detail.

Secondly, and after two or three years, when profits began
to flow, we would buy a derelict farm and build a large
broiler and pig-breeding unit, and urge local farmers to rear
the pigs, and also to grow all the foodstuffs possible for
servicing the central units. A central unit of small farm
machinery would be set up to facilitate the growers.

MAP OF GLENCOLUMBKILLE PARISH

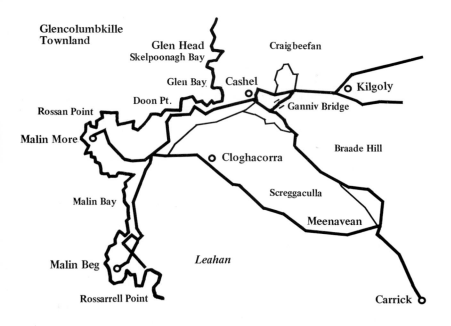

Glencolumbkille Townland

Glen Head
Skelpoonagh Bay

Craigbeefan

Glen Bay

Cashel

Kilgoly

Doon Pt.

Ganniv Bridge

Rossan Point

Malin More

Cloghacorra

Braade Hill

Malin Bay

Screggaculla

Meenavean

Malin Beg

Leahan

Rossarrell Point

Carrick

BELFAST

DUBLIN

SHANNON

CORK

Brigid and John McDyer

(Left to right) Alec, Charlie, Hugh and James McDyer; early 1930s

Ordination photograph, 1937

Fr. McDyer (second from left) with fellow students at Maynooth, 1932

Glencolumbkille (photo: Bord Fáilte)

Folk Museum (photo: Bord Fáilte)

School playground, Glencolumbkille, 1982 (photo: Steve MacDonogh)

Finally, we would use profits to buy up and recondition derelict farms and rent them out at low rates to newly-weds or returned emigrants with the option to buy.

Such was our scheme and in the conditions of those days it made much sense. Of course, my adviser could not promote it because the bureaucratic system to which he belonged frowned upon any radical initiative by its field advisers. I informed James Dillon, the then Minister for Agriculture, of the scheme and then went up to Dublin to discuss it with him. He told me he would back it provided I submitted it to the Irish Agricultural Organisation Society (IAOS), and got clearance from them.

Officials of different kinds began to flock down to Glencolumbkille and after eight months the scheme got the go-ahead from the IAOS with the wry comment of Dr. Henry Kennedy, the Secretary, that "it was the best of a bad lot". I drove to Dublin with glee and abandon to meet James Dillon. But I returned much more slowly. He had changed his mind and could not grant-aid the scheme because in it there would not be enough employment. It is as well that I cannot recall what I said because it was probably unprintable anyway. To this day I do not know whether James Dillon was speaking for himself or whether the cold hand of senior civil servants had intervened to stifle an independent and radical initiative.

During this time, aided by Michael Burke, I busied myself with three other grant-aided schemes which would benefit sheep-farming, the traditional type of farming. After several meetings I failed to convince the farmers even though several parish councillors were supporting me. It was at these meetings I began to realise how difficult it was for a local councillor to hold forth trenchantly, because the whole community was so closely knit by marriage and blood-relationships that it took a special brand of moral courage for one of their number to harangue an audience of in-laws and close neighbours. That I was a priest did not quite help me but probably as a stranger I was given a fool's pardon because I did not know the nuances of local circumstances.

It became evident to me that in failing to grant-aid the central farm scheme, the Minister dealt a final blow to the prospects of the other schemes being accepted by local farmers. In a word — my credibility was being eroded. How I silently screamed for just one word of encouragement!

* * *

Having paid off all its expenses the community hall began to make profits from dances, dramas and bazaars. We devoted these profits to purchasing land for a community park, and to other amenities. The park has since been so developed by the local GAA that it is considered one of the best playing parks in County Donegal.

Both park and hall provided us with a base for another effort to stimulate agriculture and home crafts. We launched "The Glencolumbkille Agricultural and Industrial Show".

Being a farmer's son, my first concern was for the proper utilisation of land. Aware of the innate skills of local people, I aimed that the show should stimulate pride in farming achievement, needlework and home baking. Our council and several others worked with might and main to make it a success. The show was held on the last Wednesday in August and our costs were covered by the entrance fee and the show dance.

The park was allotted to agricultural exhibits and to cattle and sheep competitions. Dogs were exhibited in their several categories. Clay pigeon shooting and horse-jumping were laid on as special attractions. Jim Doherty, Mick Byrne, Patrick Gillespie, John Heeney and Jimmy Carr ran the various events like clockwork, whilst Bridget McShane closed her public house and allowed us to use her licence on the open field. In the hall, exhibits ranging from oaten bread to iced cakes, and every conceivable type of knitwear and crochet, as well as a variety of vegetables and flower displays were packed in. Mrs. McGinley, Nan Lyons, Mary Murphy and Frances Gillespie ran it well. On the stage we had a live tableau of women operating all the local crafts of spinning, carding, knitting, crochet and hand embroidery. Magees of Donegal and Gaeltarra Éireann added immense colour to the exhibits, and the Donegal County Committee of Agriculture could not have been more helpful.

I approached in turn the American Ambassador, Sybil Connolly — a fashion designer — and Eamonn de Valera, then Leader of the Opposition in the Dáil, to open the show on its three initial years. These personalities certainly drew the crowds, and visitors came from all over South-West Donegal.

As I conducted Mr. de Valera through the packed hall he remarked to me "If only rural Ireland could see this, then all would be well".

It is interesting to note the divisive influence of politics in a community. On the year in which I had Mr. de Valera open the show several people grumbled because they did not share his politics.

However, I balanced this out by inviting General Mulcahy to open one of the feiseanna which we had instituted.

It seemed to me that a new and revealing dimension had been unveiled in Glencolumbkille. The mass involvement of a retiring, isolated community gave a sense of achievement and of pride, whilst their latent Irish courtesy in the inter-action with the influx of strangers surfaced with a natural dignity.

Paddy McGinley remarked to me "I never thought we would attract so many people to Glencolumbkille", but John Heeney expressed the community pride better when he said, "Father, I was once embarrassed to admit that I was from Glencolumbkille, because people might ask me 'Where is that place?' — Now I am no longer embarrassed".

When the first horticultural co-operative and the first hand-knitting co-operative were set up (of which more later), we considered that the show had done its work and we closed it down. Wisdom comes with experience, and often since then I have regretted the decision. The show was making people more aware of their own abilities in agri-culture or in crafts than any other promotion.

It was clear that if we were serious about building a future for the people of Glencolumbkille, amongst our primary objectives must be the provision of a new school and clinic. The old school was grossly inadequate and in a very poor state of repair, and after making a nuisance of myself I got it condemned. The standard local contribution to the cost of a new school was one-third of the total, but I knew that this was beyond our means. I saw the head man at the Department of Education, argued that this level of contribution was an unrealistic imposition on a community like ours, and then staged a walk-out when I felt I was getting nowhere. After the lapse of some weeks while tempers cooled, a more equitable arrangement was agreed and the school was built. Provision of the clinic proved much easier, as Donegal County Council was very amenable.

By now members of the parish council were getting old, and were not being replaced with new blood. They had worked very hard, especially during the years of my association with them and helped me wonderfully by advice and action. In our time we had built a hall, we had installed electricity, we had bought a park, we had made a nuisance of ourselves until we had our roads tarmacadamed, we had a clinic built, and we had a new school built. But the council had encountered a certain veiled hostility and sometimes jealousy. When the first co-operative was commenced, they considered that their work was done. How wrong we all were!

None of the younger generation seemed anxious to take up council posts. It was with a heavy heart I realised that I was alone, but the dream and determination were as great as ever. I decided that I would make one last attempt to come to terms with agriculture in Glencolumbkille.

In 1962 I attempted to get the Land Commission to subdivide our mountain commonages to provide each smallholder with about seventy acres of mountain. This could be converted into reasonably good grassland and would give a chance to the more progressive farmers to better their lot. As it was, the sheep were so undernourished that their mortality rate and that of lambs was far too high.

Officials from the Land Commission came down, but true to form, they would not subdivide if there were one or two dissenters, and each commonage had a few objectors so the officials folded their maps and went home.

Then it began to dawn on me that we should try to make a

virtue out of a necessity. If the land for sheep-grazing were already in communes, why not endeavour to persuade as many of the smallholders as possible to communise temporarily the farms which were all too small to be economic. There would then be no question of sub-dividing the existing mountain commonages into comparatively small little strips of about seventy acres each, but instead, the mountains would be divided into two groups, one for those who wanted to communise their little farms and one for those who did not wish to do so.

Of course, the word commune has uncomfortable overtones in Ireland and Western Europe for those whose material interests are well served by our present economic system. But our commune would have few Stalinist connotations. Ours would not be forced on the people; the landowners would decide for themselves, assisted by a hired agronomist. Ours would not be state-owned, but would be owned by the participants. Ours was based on the Irish traditional *meitheal* which reflected the Christian concept of helping your neighbour. Ours would treat its weakest member with the same dignity as the strongest. Ours would be used to produce that for which the terrain was best suited, and with such a strong emphasis on good husbandry that each single acre would be treated to produce its full potential. A technocrat would be hired by the owners of the commune who, in committee, would advise him on local conditions. Moreover, farmers would be deflected from spending most of their working year in non wealth-producing occupations in hand-won turbary, or fodder for one cow, or in hand-cultivation of sufficient potatoes for the domestic table. Instead of these non wealth-producing efforts the farmers would be employed on large farm-units which would show a profit, and they would be paid agricultural wages for doing so at the rate prevailing in the country.

Turf, fodder, and root crops would be produced in communal units by machine, and each home would receive all it required for free in turf, potatoes, vegetables, and milk. Moreover, sufficient vegetables would be produced for our vegetable factory. Also, the dairy herd would be utilised for the production of butter which would be marketed to members of the commune at a very cheap rate. Finally, those homes in the commune where people were too old to work, would receive a special payment equivalent to the living wage of a breadwinner.

Such was the scheme which I advanced for one hundred and thirty contiguous small farms in Glencolumbkille for a trial period of ten years. We would borrow corporately and repay corporately. The people would not be parting with their farms forever. They could withdraw after ten years if they wished, but I was sure they would not because of the increase in wealth from this intensely co-operative action.

At first my audiences were incredulous: then they were dismayed, and on the first round of meetings I knew that I had not captured either imagination or consent. Fortunately, however, there were some young men at the different meetings who were impressed, and at the crossroads meetings they sold the idea sufficiently for me to ask the Agricultural Institute and the Irish Agricultural Organisation Society (IAOS) to do a joint survey.

A report was produced which advised, among other things, that if the mountain land was properly treated we could carry six times the existing sheep population. This would be wealth indeed. They also advised that every male worker could be employed and that after the third year we could begin to employ female workers. (This advice, however positive, reflected the backward assumption that the men should have jobs first, an assumption I have never found to be justified by the evidence of ability or production.) Of the one hundred and thirty farmers originally approached, one hundred and twelve were willing to operate the plan.

I was excited. If our scheme succeeded we could eventually produce a solution for the whole problem of the small, uneconomic holding in any land. With a communal farm of fourteen thousand acres of mountain and a thousand acres of lowland, and marginal land, we would be amongst the largest farms in Europe. The new economy of scale would allow for efficient methods of agriculture to be employed. But I did not reckon with the cold winds of bureaucracy which were to shrivel us before we commenced.

I approached the Agricultural Credit Corporation for a loan. But the collateral required was the title deeds of every farm. I could not, and would not deliver. It was then suggested that I go for a government sponsored loan. At the meeting in the office of the Minister for Agriculture were representatives of several government departments and state-sponsored bodies. I felt quite confident because I believed that the Minister, Charles J. Haughey, was marginally in favour of my initiative and also, I was fortified with the report of the prestigious Agricultural Institute. But the most powerful bodies were against me. These were the Department of Agriculture and the Land Commission, as also was the Sugar Company for some peculiar reason. The civil servants hedged by asking for feasibility studies. I reminded them about St. Colmcille and the druids and the efforts of the druids to thwart him by calling up the mists. I said: "The druids have gone but they have left their peers behind in you boys, the senior civil servants. The modern druidical mist is your feasibility study."

Every objection could be answered in the report that I possessed. But at length one speaker arose and said that the scheme was not Christian. I erupted, and told them that while they might all be experts in several spheres, I was the only expert on Christianity present. I said "good-day, gentlemen", and walked out. The Minister followed me and advised me that a watered-down scheme would be required because the departments were going to play tug-o-war with the original scheme. An anaemic scheme was produced towards which Mr. Haughey made a special grant. From it eventually emerged "The Glencolumbkille Sheep Farmers' Co-Operative".

It was my second clash with government departments, but it was not to be my last. Ever since, I have been plagued with thoughts that my methods were wrong. Perhaps months should have been spent in smoothing down the feelings of the Land Commission and ensuring that even if the scheme worked and spread, they would have no cause to be threatened in their raison d'être. Perhaps I should not have given an interview to *The Irish Times* before I met the Department of Agriculture and the Land Commission. This was bound to raise hackles. However, I saw no value for the ordinary people in codes of secrecy which are so valued by bureaucrats. Anyhow, I am such a rebel against state paternalism that I did not feel it necessary to consult and get agreement in advance. I was wrong: the state bodies held the key to the purse.

Some people so admired the freshness of our new plan that they advised me to go to America on a collection tour. I replied that if I mentioned the word commune over there I might be placed on the next plane home. Someone, less seriously, suggested that I go to Russia and collect roubles there. But with tongue in cheek I replied that I did not know the language.

I grieved for the gallant Glencolumbkille people who were prepared to embark on such a new scheme. And I have ever since grieved that it did not at least get a trial, because I am convinced that it could have solved everywhere the problem of the small uneconomic farm, whilst retaining the dignity and the title of its owner. Our ignorance is a part of our oppression! The forces opposed to Christ's vision of justice and equality do not lurk only on distant shores, or within some alien race: every nation has its poor and its powerful.

Although that period of my life was dominated by intense pressures of work and fundamental disappointments, one small incident made such an impression on my mind that it is amongst the sharpest of my recollections. I was driving to Dublin early one morning. A skylark was busy on the road in front of me, determined to get his morning roughage. He took no notice of me, and I could not avoid him: one moment he was busy in life, the next he was dead.

CHAPTER IX

For some years in the late nineteen-fifties events moved at an ever quickening pace. During the time I was working on my final attempt at a worthwhile agricultural initiative, I had been busy with other things as well. We had no piped water supply; without it we could not give the community the opportunity of twentieth century amenities. There was no opposition from the local people, some of whom, however, would have been quite content if they had had village pumps erected. I was against this and wrote to the county secretary asking him to be adamant that when water was supplied it should be brought right inside the houses. He agreed.

But the main problem was to have the plan initiated. Here we were in competition with other areas in Donegal which were larger and more prestigious; Glencolumbkille was very far down on the list of priorities. However, Michael O'Donnell, our local county councillor, was a powerful advocate for us. One day I called on him with a few new arguments to strengthen our case, only to discover that he had already gone to a county council meeting. I chased him down to Lifford where he was attending the meeting. He listened to me, and then to my surprise and embarrassment he asked me into the council chamber where he requested the chairman to give me a hearing. This unusual request was grudgingly granted. It was obvious that the chairman did not like it which embarrassed me further, but he allowed me four minutes. I do not recall what I said but within three months a water scheme was commenced in Glencolumbkille. I attributed our success not to eloquence but to gall.

But the scheme was too small. It accommodated only thirty houses. There was a vast spread of houses scattered around the hillsides and the valleys which had no supply, and which no county council in its senses would attempt to service because of the costs. Fr. Seamus McGeehan of Dublin told me of an organisation called World University Service which involved university students from more developed countries assisting in areas where there was local demand for development. He also told me of the "group water scheme" which combined communal endeavour in the installation with a substantial grant from local government to supply the fittings.

I acted immediately, and the World University Service set up their first voluntary work camp in Ireland with us. The volunteers came from seven different countries with the majority from the host country, and they were all excellent. They set up five different camps in Glencolumbkille over a span of four summers during the early nineteen-sixties. The spoken language was English. Each summer, five male students came from the French universities. Though they were very good they did not seem to have the ebullient drive of the Scandinavians, the Germans, Dutch, English and Irish, and they rested quite a lot, so I requested the camp leader to divide all the workers into groups of three as they dug the trenches. "Now" said I, "place one girl with every two French students." The working capacity of the French increased spectacularly!

The work camps were financed by profits from the community hall. Local people joined the work in the evenings and supplied groceries and vegetables and a local committee organised many social gatherings. The group water schemes cost only ten pounds per house. Since then, Francis Cunningham, county councillor, has had another two water schemes completed so that now the gap is almost completely closed.

It would be unfair to assume that we had to go it completely alone in Glencolumbkille without any help from officialdom. We always found the county council and their manager to be very helpful, as were the Agricultural Institute

70

and Bord Fáilte, but I often felt that the ordinary politicians were slightly less forthcoming. This may have been due to the fact that we were prone to romp ahead with new ventures and left little kudos for the politicians to glean. This fault was entirely mine. I stuck fast to the belief that as a nation we had been reduced to dependence on the government for everything and that this attitude curbed local initiative, and could eventually result in state paternalism. The powerless don't get to make choices.

But one politician stood out in my experience — Eamonn de Valera. I decided to write to him directly as head of government because I had received so many setbacks. For several years I had spent much time careering around the country trying to attract private industry to Glencolumbkille. It was all very well for us to have the infrastructure laid on in roads, electricity and eventually water supply, but I knew we must have industry if we were to trap migration at its source. The enormous efforts we had made to establish a really intensive agricultural base had come to naught, and if we could not establish an employment base then amenities alone would not put a brake on emigration. But every established industry I visited was giving me the same answer. "Glencolumbkille is too far away: you have no trained labour, and we are not strong enough to set up an ancillary industry there." I brought particular pressure on Gaeltarra Éireann who were supposed to be responsible for development in our Gaeltacht area. There was a similar answer here: "later on".

I knew that this answer had been given to the parish council some time before I arrived so I sat down and wrote a memorandum to the Taoiseach which I captioned as "the twenty-two curses of Glencolumbkille". I pointed out that we had removed quite a few of these curses but I asked him to give Gaeltarra a little push to establish an industry in Glencolumbkille. I heard afterwards that Mr. de Valera was impressed, chiefly because I advanced a constructive proposal by which each "curse" could be lifted. I had been afraid that he would not get the opportunity of reading my memorandum so I took the precaution of sending a copy to his wife as well.

The result was quite startling. Within a week he sent me down three of his own trusted men before, as he said, "the civil servants would get at me". One of these, Mr. Tod Andrews, offered me an answer to one of my "curses" on the spot. This was a contract to supply two thousand tons of hand-won turf to Bord na Móna each year, which would benefit the family homes. This was, however, rejected by the people of Glencolumbkille because, as they told me, it was only seasonal work and would upset their receipt of dole.

A further result of Mr. de Valera's taking an interest in us was that within months Glencolumbkille's first factory was set up. It was built by Gaeltarra Éireann who had hitherto been reluctant to become involved, and on the opening day politicians and officials made their speeches, but I was never asked to say a word. When I was asked why I had been muted, I could not resist the rude reply: "when crows begin to sing, blackbirds keep quiet".

But progress was made and I was elated. It really boosted the local morale, and local people knew that at last one bridge had been crossed into the difficult area of industrial development. The factory was particularly suited to Glencolumbkille because its product, Donegal tweed, in its various phases, had been a home craft in Glencolumbkille for generations. In December 1954 all this skill was gathered together under one roof to hand-loom the very updated and marketable version of the fabric.

I met Jimmy Boyle and Pete Gillespie on their way to the factory the first week. Already it seemed to me that the defeated droop had gone from their shoulders and a new spring had come into their step. "Man dear, Father" said one of them in his best Donegal accent, "it's great to be sure of your work every day." Gradually improvements were made to the homes of several employees, and one could feel the sense of dignity in the glen. The unspoken thought was "we have not been forgotten". Most exciting of all was the return of two emigrants from England with their wives and families and their employment in the factory right away.

There were about thirty people employed between weavers

and menders, and the factory carried on production for nineteen years from 1954 until 1973 when Gaeltarra Éireann became interested in producing Donegal tweed from power looms instead of hand looms. They concentrated all their power looms in Kilcar and the Glencolumbkille factory was closed. I was sorry that all this expertise in handwoven tweed was made redundant. I would have taken a stand against it, but as the workers were unionised I could not interfere. However, Magees of Donegal still employ some hand weavers locally.

From now on I resolved that I would not demean myself by going around the country with a "rice bowl" endeavouring to entice industry to set up in our area. If I had to approach the head of government to have our first industry set up, henceforeward we would commence industries ourselves. At this time I also had a very socialist dream which, unfortunately, was to remain a dream. In a low-resource area such as ours I felt that the profits of any enterprise should be owned by the people, and utilised for the good of the people. If they were scooped up by the owners of private enterprises the people of the locality would never attain any status greater than wage-earners, and would never have the financial muscle to carve out their own communal destiny.

My original objection to a community becoming totally dependent on the state and the good will of politicians and bureaucrats was now augmented by a new objection, and this was that no community should become dependent on the good will of private enterprise. I was conscious that I was travelling along the road towards radical socialism and that the ideal result was a united community with the goal of communal economic independence, by which people could carve out their own destiny in their own way.

That the dream did not come to fruition is all too true, but this was not for want of gritty endeavour. At least we opened the door to what I considered a very Christian solution. May other, and more worthy hands push the door wide open to see the sunlit vision of the Utopia beyond. I make no apology to private enterprise. It plays a vital role in the economy of the state, and entrepreneurs taking risks with their capital are entitled to a just reward as long as they fully acknowledge the sweat of their employees.

But my dream differed radically from private enterprise. Mine was community enterprise through which the curse of dependence on the investor and the bureaucrat would be lifted so that the future could be planned in dignity and equality. Infrastructure was established in this way with comparative ease but setting up an industrial and tourist base proved to be a great deal more difficult.

CHAPTER X

My strategy was to build a chain of small industries funded by the shareholding of the local people; the profits of the first two industries would prime the creation of other small factories, until a cordon enclosed the community to trap emigration and farm redundancy at its source.

First I began to gather information about co-operatives. The Irish Agricultural Organisation Society (IAOS) and General Costello of the Irish Sugar Company were very helpful. The one gave me much information and literature about the structure and mechanism of a co-operative as a practical and legal entity. The other gave me added enthusiasm concerning co-operatives as a means to create industry independent of the bureaucrats and politicians.

At this time I had the honour to serve for a few years on the national committee of the IAOS or what is now the Irish Co-operative Organisation Society. Here I felt somewhat isolated, because though the committee was composed of extremely able and dedicated people, the majority of them seemed to be representing large farming co-operatives and their ancillary industries. That was fair enough, but it was a far cry from the small multi-purpose chain of co-operatives which I had in mind. With wry humour I used to think to myself that if I intruded on their deliberations with a dissertation on the marketing difficulties of a knitting co-operative, I would be received in stony silence. I would ask myself did Count Plunkett in his pioneering role in Irish co-operatives intend that such agricultural co-operatives should be the preserve of the wealthy, the progressives, and those who owned large farms. I was sure not, but it was natural that his crusade would be utilised first of all by the strong who were quick to see its advantages, whilst the organisation of the weaker two-thirds was left to the isolated enthusiastic spirits in each community. Was it to be always this way?

Of course I was acutely aware that any co-operative project must have at least the promise of economic viability. This was vital and had to remain paramount. But there was another dimension and that was the social dimension, and in the hurly-burly of productivity and profits this aspect was apt to be neglected or forgotten. After all, co-operatives represented the amalgamation of individuals with common problems to attain common goals for the benefit of all participants. Consequently, I felt that a co-operative should rally primarily to the aid of its bona fide weakest members and, if at all possible, should endeavour to stimulate the economic growth and the services within its own catchment area. This would prevent the dependence of the many on the powerful. The real antagonists of co-operatives were always those who tried to monopolise and exploit for their own private gain. The teachings of Christ favour co-operation and socialism, and His enemies were those who were abusing power.

Amidst all these thoughts, the limited but untapped agricultural potential of Glencolumbkille still nagged at my mind. Colm McGuire, a progressive farmer with a small acreage, had over the years been growing vegetables successfully for marketing. I joined him by growing vegetables on a tiny piece of parochial land, in order to show surrounding farmers that vegetable marketing could be a viable proposition and could enable them to wrest considerable earnings from their farms. But if they all commenced to grow fresh vegetables the market in the villages around us would soon become saturated. Then I thought of Dublin and I transported a car load of fresh vegetables to the Dublin market and sold them. I can still see the astonishment of faces as they saw this priest barge into the market with his crate of wares! But I knew this would be no solution — transport was too costly.

I had read a lot about General Michael J. Costello of the Irish Sugar Company and the great work he was doing in the processing of home grown vegetables. I consulted him in 1961 and he gave me hope. General Costello was an outstanding man of courage and foresight and I believe he will be remembered as a great Irishman of this century. He stood apart like a colossus among all those who have been involved in state-sponsored bodies before or since. He was the champion of the small farmer and with his incisive and forthright manner he seemed to me to discharge all his vast responsibilities in an orderly and efficient way. Perhaps he was influenced in this by his brilliant army career.

In our discussion I mentioned my plan to set up a co-operative factory for the processing of vegetables. I doubted whether our community could supply sufficient vegetables but felt that the communities around us for a radius of several miles would almost certainly participate. He told me that the minimum required would be two hundred acres of vegetables. It was obvious that he was keen to revitalise the small farms and he told me that if we commenced the Sugar Company would help in every way possible and even assume responsibility for management, quality control, marketing and training of workers.

Meetings were held and the proposition was put to the local people. It was well received. The scheme had a two-pronged purpose: it would benefit the local farmers and it would create places in industry for some of their children. A committee was formed. General Costello even came down and addressed meetings in neighbouring communities. One of the most important things he did for us was to take thirty of our young men and women for training in food processing in Sugar Company factories. Soil surveys were carried out, which did not prove very encouraging but the worst blow was that most of the farmers in neighbouring communities refused to take growing contracts. By that time I thought the scheme would come to nought.

It was then that the people of our community showed their mettle. At a general meeting in Carrick, where the late John McGinley played a notable part, it was resolved tumultuously that the people of the parish of Glencolumbkille would grow two hundred acres of vegetables. John McGinley, a businessman in Carrick who had returned from England, was a magnificent public relations officer. He was here, there, and everywhere. Not only had he totted up the acreage but he organised a campaign for share capital and accumulated eight thousand pounds between Kilcar, Carrick, and Glencolumbkille.

From then on there seemed no turning back. Peadar O'Donnell organised a meeting of the Donegal Association in Dublin, and two thousand pounds was subscribed. Meetings of the Donegal Associations in London, Birmingham, and four cities in the USA were organised. In a sixteen day tour of America I addressed meetings in New York, Philadelphia, Chicago and Boston, inviting my audiences to take up shares in our new co-operative factory. Bernie McGinley, my housekeeper, who had become deeply involved in our community efforts, and her sister, Una, a local teacher, had done much of the preparatory work. All the same I had many nervous doubts as I flew across the Atlantic; but these were dispelled by the efficiency of the Irish-Americans and their determination to do everything possible to welcome a native son.

At each city I was greeted by a welcoming party and brought to the home of my host. In Chicago the schedule was so tight that I was rushed at high speed from the airport to a radio studio and a live and rather breathless interview started almost before I could sit into my chair. I shall never forget the immense work done by the various officials of the Donegal Associations. In Boston Mrs Daly seemed to have lived on the phone for several days before the meeting; she even tried to arrange for me to meet Cardinal Cushing, but unfortunately he was ill. And amongst the names that stand out in my memory are Willie Cunningham of New York, Michael Heaney and Neil Byrne of Philadelphia, and Michael Cunningham, John Byrne, Monsignor Cunningham, Brigid O'Gara and Mrs Christy Doogan of Chicago.

In addition to their efficiency, the kindness and hospitality of these Irish Americans was quite extraordinary. On the night I arrived in Chicago there were no less than three house parties laid on for me, and I didn't roll into bed until two in the morning. And I was showered with gifts wherever I went. The Irish at home are considered friendly and hospitable, but we have immense returns to make to our cousins in the USA.

Eighteen thousand pounds were collected in America, and those who rallied to our support in providing share capital have the comfort of knowing that they have ensured the permanence of fifty homes in our community and the circulation of a minimum of a quarter of a million pounds annually in wages. My final memory is of the man in Boston who came up to me after my address, clapped me on the shoulder, and said: "Father, this is the greatest news since Brian Boru!"

The first crop of vegetables was grown. The day the factory opened was dull, wet and chill: real November weather. A pale yellow sun hung uselessly low over the hilltops giving the glens a livid, sinister aspect. The new factory was opened at eleven with great ceremony, by Seán Lemass, and the wheels of machinery began to roll.

But now the blows of adversity began to fall thick and fast. John McGinley, on whom I had relied so heavily, died suddenly. Much of the acreage pledged for growing proved illusory because some people were afraid to lose the dole if they grew too much.

This question of the dole really annoyed me, and I confronted Seán Lemass about it and wrote an article in the *Irish Independent*. My theme was "let them have their dole until such time as their confidence is restored and then, having acquired a new sense of dignity in their farming they would cheerfully relinquish their unemployment assistance". I also felt certain that the reason local people opted out and vast numbers in neighbouring communities would not participate, was fear of losing unemployment benefit. The situation, to my mind, reflected a crazy attitude on the part of government, because here we were trying to uplift the small farmers and there was no magnanimity among those in power. But, I suppose, we were so isolated that we could not be taken seriously.

Many farmers would cheerfully rent us land and though we were forced to rent to keep up supplies, it proved to be a financial drain on the co-operative. An agricultural adviser did great work to ensure good quality, but then in our second year, a freak storm in June wiped out our total acreage of beans. After the third year, some of our most reliable farmers began to run into rotational difficulties: they dare not plant the same crop on the same land year after year but their acreage of arable land was tiny. It seemed that we were doomed to failure. But our manager and our committee fought back and obtained large growing contracts in the fertile land of East Donegal. Nevertheless, despite the best efforts of management, committee, and staff, we were constantly making a loss. The Sugar Company took out an equity but still the losses mounted.

After ten years, the manager, Mr. Jarlath Morris, told me that we could not continue. If we were to become competitive we would require sophisticated machinery costing about three quarters of a million pounds. I remember this meeting with him well because I would not accept defeat. In particular, I would not accept the redundancy of fifty or sixty well-trained and dedicated staff.

"Look," said I, "the sea is all around us and it must have lots of fish. Take a few months off and learn all you can about fish-processing and marketing." He did it and he did it well. In a period of three years we gradually phased out vegetables, built new buildings and installed new machinery, and fish-processing has been successfully operated ever since.

But, of course, this was done at the cost of the co-operative losing control because a sizeable capital investment was required. A small company was formed and Donegal Fish Ltd. provided the investment. Erin Foods and the old co-operative had equal shares and Gaeltarra Éireann provided ten percent. I have no regrets, because workers are still employed and in even greater numbers, and I have been able to protect the money of our original shareholders.

Our next factory did not have quite the same convulsions, but it also has had a period of deathly sickness. My thinking always has been that if an industry has a chance of survival in a fairly remote rural district, it must be based on local raw materials or at least local, traditional skill. This had been the reasoning behind the Gaeltarra Éireann factory for hand-woven Donegal tweed. It was the same with the vegetable processing factory and its successor, the fish-processing factory.

Now I turned to knitting. Mrs. Mary Ann Gillespie, a very excellent knitter, asked my advice about having a hand-knitting promotion commenced. Knowing her worth as a manageress, I advised her to commence a hand-knitting co-operative in which I would give her every possible help, short of knitting myself. Previously, having promoted boxing tournaments in Glencolumbkille I had become known in other communities as the "boxing priest". Later, I had become known as the "vegetable priest", but I did not relish becoming known as the "knitting priest".

This hand-knitting and hand-crochet co-operative was started because knitting and crochet were so traditional, and several workers were of the opinion that they were not receiving enough pay for their work. We knew that, as a co-operative, we could pay more. Only about sixty knitters joined in 1964. The remainder preferred to stay with the well-established businesses for which they had been knitting. Morever, our manageress insisted on a very high standard which deterred some. Our competitors began to chase us in price, and thus we have been able to benefit not only the co-operative knitters but also the workers outside the co-operative through raising prices.

The presence of the vacant old school which we had had replaced by a new one began to give me ideas. Could we have a small industry established there? I had a vague idea that some form of machine-knitting might be established. I invited three businessmen to meet me in Dublin and asked their advice. Several other suggestions were made but machine-knitting was adopted.

I drove home speedily. A committee was formed; three thousand pounds were collected locally in share capital: I was requested to deal with the manager of the vacated school with a view to purchasing the building. But I was the manager of the old school; I sought independent advice, sat down with myself, wearing two hats, and an equitable price was proposed which was agreeable to both parties.

We refused to deal with Gaeltarra Éireann in the acquisition of a grant for machinery and extension, because they were already competitors of ours and we deemed it unethical that a competitor should be the arbiter of a grant.

Messrs. Pallas of Dublin took up a minority shareholding and the Industrial Development Authority supplied the initial grant in 1966, the year the factory was opened. We had achieved another source of employment in Glencolumbkille.

CHAPTER XI

When our local reporter, Willie Cunningham, reported my words about "the five curses of Glencolumbkille", I had reacted with some shock at such public exposure. It was only with the passage of time that I came to recognise the immense contribution he was making and were it not for him and the publicity of a generally sympathetic press, both provincial and national, our task would have been more difficult. We often criticise the media for filling our papers with bad news and news of violence, frustration, confrontation and sorrow. But my experience of Irish papers has always been that if there is a story of hope or endeavour they will certainly give it sympathetic exposure. So too will Irish television and overseas newspapers and television. In several countries, even as far distant as Japan, there was reportage of the struggle being waged in our community. This publicity involved me personally and I gradually became inundated with invitations to speak.

It was certainly not part of my strategy to dissipate my energies by travelling hither and thither to address meetings, but I disliked refusing and so, over a period of six or seven years, I reckon that I addressed meetings in thirty out of the thirty-two counties of Ireland, and also some in Britain, Holland and France.

By far the most concentrated area for meetings was in the West of Ireland, particularly in Mayo and Galway. This was natural because at that time these areas were suffering from the same heavy emigration as West Donegal. Charlestown in County Mayo was one of the first places which invited me to speak.

There was rarely much variation in my message. It was simply this. People must not wait on governments and bureaucrats or strangers to come and improve their lot. They must do it the hard way and that was to unite into community co-operatives and embark on a job creation spree. At a trade union meeting I urged their vast membership to do the same. Naturally, I used our experiences in Glencolumbkille to stimulate the audience.

I shall never forget the eagerness and kindness of these people from the disadvantaged areas in the West. How I wished that I could have given more concentrated help to them but all I could do was speak and pass on because at the end of each meeting there would be, almost inevitably, a delegation from some other village or town asking me to give an address and I could not find it in my heart to refuse. In the early stages, and after a series of addresses, an umbrella organisation called the "Charlestown Committee" was formed. The connotation of this was deemed too parochial and the name was changed to "The Defence of the West". At this time the Western bishops formally requested my bishop to release me for a period of intense promotion and organisation in the West. At a large and enthusiastic meeting in County Cork where I shared the platform with Peadar O'Donnell and General Costello, Peadar, who was well known for his leftist views, turned to look at me and said: "I do not know whether I have moved to the right or the Church has moved to the left!"

Neither my bishop nor myself was enthusiastic about over-involvement. Certainly, from my personal point of view, I did not want the campaign in Glencolumbkille to suffer, and consequently a compromise was reached, that I would attend two meetings per week in Mayo or Galway. This I did for almost three years from 1965-68.It certainly sapped time and energy because all the meetings were public, and no matter how distant the venue was from home I always returned to Glencolumbkille in the small hours, conscious as I was that my first duty was the spiritual care of my own people.

But the effort in Mayo and Galway was too dissipated to

be a success. There was no chance to return to any location and consolidate. This was almost entirely my fault, for I felt I could not disappoint those who came to ask me to speak in far away, widely scattered districts.

One of the most interesting features of the campaign was the reaction of the Fianna Fáil party. The pundits in headquarters did not like it. The packed meetings, the widespread eagerness of the people, the growing clamour for a better deal for the West, all conspired to raise hackles in Merrion Street and Mount Street, so much so that instructions were circulated to the local party committees to have nothing to do with the movement. I personally knew of one important civil servant who was so enthusiastic about our movement that he spoke from our platform, but the warning came quickly from Dublin that he must cease forthwith. The government apparently did not like the criticism it was receiving as a result of our activities. Indeed, I remember being quietly advised by one minister that I should absent myself from the meetings in the West because, said he "such areas should be allowed to find their own level of depopulation."

There was an opinion current at the time that we should organise a march on Dublin to persuade the government to halt the neglect of the West, and if this failed, that we should form a Western political party. Ironically, those in power were saved from further embarrassment by my personal intervention. As a priest I would not take part in party politics because I viewed them as divisive. As an individual I regarded the main parties as opportunist. Looking back, I am now sorry that I did not agree to organise a march on Dublin from the West of Ireland. At least it would have drawn attention to the pressure building up behind the proposal to form a Western political party. It is almost certain that the intensity of this campaign in the West did highlight the neglected condition of the more remote counties and certainly galvanised the government into making a greater effort on their behalf.

An interesting episode took place at this time. We had been campaigning for the government to set up pilot areas in the more neglected districts which, in the words of Peadar O'Donnell, would be "bridgeheads of hope". Continuing our drum-fire of agitation, we eventually received an invitation from the government to meet them in Dublin. I suppose it is a measure of our bellicose attitude that we truculently insisted that they meet us on our own territory. A compromise was reached by which they met us in a courthouse in Carrick-on-Shannon. When we arrived at the venue we found a senior official of the Department of Agriculture already seated on the rostrum as chairman. I rudely queried his right to sit there, saying that the chairman should be freely elected and an embarrassing moment ensued but I was eventually mollified by my own people. At the luncheon break I proposed to go home because we seemed to be making no progress but Peadar O'Donnell quietened me with the remark that even if we did not seem to be making progress, it was a great achievement to get these civil servants "out from under the stones". After a period, the Fianna Fáil government announced, as a political decision, the formation of twelve pilot areas along the whole Western half of the country, but they were so widely scattered that they made little impact on the general rural population.

Sadly I disengaged myself from the lecture tours, principally because I was physically unable to bear the pressure but also because there was a danger that the momentum would be lost in Glencolumbkille. It will not be easy to forget the kindness of this great people in Mayo and Galway, nor the patriotism of such men as James Donoghue, Sean McEvoy, Fr. Malachy Stephens and Peadar O'Donnell. If the West continues to provide people of this calibre, then all will be well.

But now another national problem was looming on the horizon which could affect our destiny for generations, for it became apparent that there was a movement afoot to expand the EEC to include both Britain and Ireland. Obviously this would be a major decision for Ireland. Britain was our main customer, especially for food and it was obvious that if Britain joined the EEC and we did not, access to our principal customer would be jeopardised. If, on the other hand, we joined the EEC with the British, we would no longer be tied to the traditional cheap food policy of the

British governments but would have a much wider market at our disposal on favourable terms. There was therefore a very cogent and appealing argument in favour of our joining, and this was made more attractive still by the opportunity of a free flow of capital, labour, and goods within the countries belonging to the EEC. The bait was held out to us in the West of Ireland, that here was an opportunity for having our country rapidly industrialised. Finally a note of warning was sounded that if the British joined the EEC and we did not, then we could bid goodbye forever to our aspiration to regain the last colony of the British in the North-East and reunite our island.

The two principal political parties in the Republic avidly espoused the cause of entry into the EEC. They were joyously joined by the large farmers and by a considerable segment of the civil service. One could certainly sympathise with their attitude for a veritable bonanza was promised for the large farmers and there was a hope that Ireland would quickly become industrialised by the injection of foreign capital.

But there was a tiny group of us who considered that in the general euphoria for full membership of the EEC, the major political parties and the large farmers did not sufficiently think the implications through. Naturally, I was worried about the fate of the small farmers, and I also wondered whether there would be such a stampede of foreign capital to Ireland as had been envisaged. And should it materialise then all the elements of republicanism within me were revolted at the prospect of such a take-over.

The few of us who did endeavour to set the alarm bells ringing were geographically isolated and as a result it was difficult to have cohesion. Nevertheless, we plodded along in company with a few members of the Labour party but we had not a chance against the combined weight of the two principal parties and the large farmers. We cast doubt on the immediate industrialisation of Ireland: we are at the far Western perimeter of the market and capital was usually centrifugal; we worried about the life span of our adolescent Irish industries; we doubted if the large farmers would enjoy a continuing bonanza in dairy products, particularly since the red lights of surplus production were already flashing from the Continent. We prophesied the slow demise of our own independence, life style, and culture, and the gradual demise of the small family farm. One particular speech I delivered in Monaghan on the threat to the small farms of the West was denounced in the Dáil the following day by the then Taoiseach, Jack Lynch.

We did not advocate a complete aloofness from the Common Market. We maintained that a country as young as Ireland should seek only associate membership, but we were told that the Eurocrats were surprisingly compassionate and socialist-minded, and that our true home was in Europe because of our so-called historical connections with the Continent.

In our puny efforts to persuade the Irish people to stop and think, I remember one or two very interesting encounters. The late General Tom Barry (whose patriotism nobody can question) was invited by our organisers to a news conference in Dublin. He took me aside and advised me not to spend too much energy fighting a cause for the Irish people. "We boast that we fought the British for seven hundred and fifty years until we finally got rid of them out of twenty-six counties. I say that it is a shame that it took us so long, and the reason is that we never united. Look at the rebellion of 1798," he said, "most of the country stood by while there was such carnage at Vinegar Hill. Look at 1916 — there were many guns in Ireland then, and if everyone had but fired a shot in the air they would have kept fresh contingents of the British from assailing Dublin and extinguishing the fire of freedom that flickered in the GPO. I tell you, Father, don't worry too much about the EEC. The Irish people are not worth fighting for." I think really that he must have been deeply disappointed by the direction events had taken in Ireland since the War of Independence, and out of kindness he wished me to be spared similar disappointment.

On another occasion I was invited to a television debate on the EEC as part of the anti-Market team. The debate was in the form of a court proceeding, with a judge and all the trimmings. For a year or two I had been trying to prise a grant from the Ministry for the Gaeltacht for some holiday homes we had built, but the Minister refused to pay the last three thousand pounds because, he said, we were not speaking enough Irish.

During the television debate the judge intervened to ask me to put, in one or two sentences, my principal objection. "Well" said I, "our government will gradually lose some of their power for making their own decisions. This is unfortunate because our Dublin government is usually benevolent, but they are not always benevolent" said I "because they owe me three thousand pounds away back in Glencolumbkille." The following week I received a cheque from the Ministry without comment.

I regretted the result of the referendum on the EEC but I had to accept it. When asked about the result, I transposed the famous words of Sir Edward Gray and I said, "The lamps of true patriotism are going out all over Ireland tonight and we shall not see them kindled again in our lifetime".

Ireland has been a member of the EEC since January 1973, and in that time the plight of the small farmers, the prices of consumer goods, and the redundancy of so many workers, have given many more people reason to regret the result of the referendum.

CHAPTER XII

In my early years in Glencolumbkille I had received wonderful help from the parish council which led me through all the procedural machinery involved in installing electric light, water supply, improvement of roads, and having a dispensary built. But by 1962 it had declined through lack of new blood. Then, in 1964, it was decided that as each co-operative was formed it would expand its interests to deal with community development in general, and thus take over the function previously served by the parish council. At this stage, of course, there were only two co-operatives, the vegetable growing and processing co-operative and the hand-knitting co-operative. The machine-knitting co-operative was to follow in 1966.

Of these, the vegetable co-operative was by far the largest and the most capitalised, with twenty-nine thousand pounds capital in ten pound shares. Eight thousand pounds of this was subscribed locally and the remainder from Dublin, London, Birmingham and the USA through the courtesy of the Donegal Associations there. The hand-knitting co-operative required minimal capital and the shares for the machine-knitting co-operative were subscribed locally. When the subscriptions were pledged, the investors met and elected an executive committee who acted as monitors of the expenditure and also as policy-makers. The manager attended their meetings as an expert adviser without a vote. The committee was replaceable each three years — one-third of the members changing every year.

I soon discovered that the executive committees were

so engrossed in the economic welfare of their own co-operatives that the members had little patience with any new proposals extraneous to their particular objective. This was perfectly understandable, given their difficult fight for survival. It is always easy to be wise after the event but I think we did make a mistake by not issuing a monthly bulletin of information. Our community was so tightly knit that this procedure was considered superfluous. On every possible occasion when I met the people publicly I tried to outline to them what we were doing and what we proposed to do, but I often found that my spoken word was misinterpreted or misunderstood, so I eventually kept quiet. This in turn was a mistake because an uninformed public is a rumour-prone public. The cut and thrust of debate and constructive criticism at an annual general meeting keeps an executive committee on their toes or can have them replaced; but we were denied all that. But now an attitude began to manifest itself which had an extremely retarding influence on the progress of the co-operatives. The people did not trouble to come out to the AGM's. We would consider ourselves lucky if we had fifteen shareholders at any AGM.

It would be unfair to blame the shareholders for this. Probably their attitude was that they had carried out their duty by becoming shareholders and it was the duty of the executive committee to do the remainder. Probably they were disillusioned by the inability of any of the three co-operatives to show a profit in their early years and as a consequence lost interest. But the Glencolumbkille community had also observed over the years the number of times that sound ideas ran up against the solid wall of bureaucratic resistance. I believe that the enthusiasm and energy of our local people were continually dampened by this great stumbling block, and some apathy and inertia crept back into our midst. They could not expect fair and responsible support from the semi-state bodies when small industrial projects foundered or were still-born for want of as little as five thousand pounds from the state. For instance, ten jobs in a cut-and-sew industry disappeared before our eyes after we had supplied the building, trained the workers, and obtained the markets. And the five thousand pound grant due to us was never repaid. These workers were re-employed in another industry which we set up, and again it was allowed to die because after we had pumped into it twenty-three thousand pounds capital we could afford no more. State officials may have their reasons for seeming indifference but their procrastination in matters relating to local initiative can wreak havoc on the morale of a community.

But I was convinced that there should be further development. We had done our best on the agricultural front and we had established a few industries. There was one local source that was as yet hardly tapped and this was the attraction of our natural surroundings in mountains, beaches, and archaeology.

I was obsessed with the fear that some strangers would come along with plenty of money and destroy the character of Glencolumbkille by instituting a type of tourist development out of character with the environment. I thought that the benefits of tourism should be spread in such a way that the local people would benefit to the greatest possible extent. Helped by a highly qualified young hotelier named Dermot Walsh, we launched a campaign for what we grandiosely called the establishment of sixty "mini-hotel" home-farm holidays.

We carefully canvassed about sixty housewives. We secured the combined help of Bord Fáilte and the ESB to organise a week's intensive instruction in catering for tourists. Nothing was left out. There was even an instruction in the proper making of beds. But evidently the people were not yet ready for this type of development: thirty people attended the course but only three accepted the challenge. This was a disappointment but I resolved I would somehow make one more effort.

In my travels I had seen the Bunratty Folk Museum and the Ulster Museum, and suddenly I became fired with the idea that we should build a West Donegal Folk Museum. Students from the faculty of architecture in University College, Dublin came down and chose a site. Pat McGinley, a local factory manager, sold me the land. Lord Moyne gave a substantial donation, many of the people of Glencolumbkille gave one day's free work; all the people of Glencolumbkille gave old period furniture and utensils and artifacts. A unit consisting of four cottages, representing the past three hundred years in West Donegal, took shape. The Glencolumbkille Folk Museum was built in three months. I had previously received outline planning permission, and on the day after Erskine Childers, Minister for Transport and Tourism, opened the complex in 1967, I received formal planning permission.

Since that time the folk museum has expanded considerably. We have built a craft shop for the sale of Irish crafts. We have built a "shebeen". The presence of a "shebeen" for the sale of spirits was a feature of the Irish countryside until about a hundred years ago. Of course there is a poteen still on display, but instead of selling its product we sell various types of home-made wine and jam and bread which is baked in the museum. We have also erected a school identical with the national schools of a hundred years ago, and we have plans for further expansion.

The folk museum is not a co-operative; it is a charitable trust, and in deference to the great efforts of the people of the parish in furnishing it, the profits are made over to them for the advancement of traditional culture and for the higher education of their more needy children, in perpetuity.

As the day trippers flocked in their hundreds to the museum and as they commented favourably on the snug little cottages, the idea began to dawn on me that we should build a number of thatched cottages with modern furnishings and conveniences. These would rent out to tourists and hopefully, the people of Glencolumbkille would somehow own them. But it was a rash hope. Nobody displayed any interest in the project and several claimed that there was no future for tourism in Glencolumbkille. Perhaps I was asking too much because even if there had been enthusiasm it is doubtful if sufficient capital could be raised.

Again Dermot Walsh came to my aid. "Let's form a company" said he. "With whom?" said I. "Quite simple" said he, "just you and me on a fifty-fifty basis." This was quite alien to my philosophy. Moreover, it was frightening because I had not a penny to spare and I am sure he had not got much more. However, we received limited accommodation from the bank. The site was bought and the work began. But we had only just started when a major blow fell. The bank refused to advance any further capital. I acted quickly. I invited Mr. Ted O'Boyle (a bank director whom I knew) to visit us and if possible to sort out the dilemma. He came and it was probably fortunate that he saw me when I was out helping the builders. In my shirt sleeves on the roadside, I outlined our problem. He courteously capitulated. Bord Fáilte entered into the spirit of enthusiasm that gripped us and gave us phased grants to supplement the borrowed capital.

It is a tribute to the Glencolumbkille builders and workmen that the first ten cottages were completed within seventeen months — probably a record for speed, and that was just in time to meet the deadline for the arrival of the tourists. This could not have been accomplished were it not for the voluntary effort of some Glencolumbkille women who came to me and offered to take charge of the interior cleaning, decorating and furnishing. I shall never forget their enthusiasm and dedication, particularly the flair displayed by Bernie McGinley. Bernie is a remarkable woman. Previously she had been quiet and retiring but she recognised the worry and the drama that was unfolding and she really discovered her own genius. She and her colleagues worked into the early morning hours to have everything ready on time. So great was her contribution that I promptly appointed her manageress of the holiday village which she directed with distinction from its inception until she got married in 1979.

But the distinction of a company director sat uneasily on me. All my efforts had been for the good of the community and I certainly did not want to have any personal gain. For me the rejection of a co-operative in tourism development was a watershed. I was confronted with a choice: should I throw in the towel and call a halt to my personal involvement or should I continue. But how could I continue if there was no longer a parish council to sustain me and if I was

94

unable to persuade the co-operative committees to expand their interests?

More small industries would be required but I knew that we would need capital to entice them into our isolated community and where would we find the money? Of course, Gaeltarra Éireann could come forward with grants but there seemed to be no local interest in initiating industry. The tourist base would have to be further expanded but my partner and I were stretched to the limit on capitalisation. Moreover, he lived a long distance from me and was not interested in expansion. Finally, and most important of all, there did not seem to be anyone who was interested. I felt frustrated and alone and I nearly made the final decision to retire from community development altogether.

There are two occasions when I find it easiest to commune with a higher power. The first is when I lie down in bed awaiting sleep. Then my conversation with Him is at its most intimate as we review the day's work. I find that my conversation usually falls under two heads: the blame that attaches to me during the day for constantly thrusting myself forward without reference to Him, and a constant litany of wants. If there is a success, I offer it to Him; if there is disaster or an unfair criticism I give it as a present from me to Him.

The other occasion is when I go away by myself to a lonely, lonely place, but it must be somewhere special to me. Did you ever sit beside a chuckling mountain stream? No, but it must be at a point where the stream is in its least garrulous mood so that the noise does not impinge too much on the consciousness. It must be at the point where the waters make a gentle murmur as they eddy their way towards the exit of some pellucid pool. High overhead there must be the song of a sky-lark and the white clouds drifting lazily across the face of the sun as they reflect the light and shade and the changing moods of the Donegal sky. Surrounded by these sights and sounds which, for me, are the most gentle, caressing and exhilarating manifestations of nature, I proceed to carry out an audit of my position and find myself anaesthetised against the harsh realities of life.

But now something dramatic happened with the arrival of

four people who shared my ideals that they should gain no personal profit but that all should be done for the community. They lined up beside me and their message was: carry on. "We will work with you" they said, "and we will share worry and responsibility." There was P.J. Daly, a returned emigrant, who was consumed with nationalism. He found a job as a mechanical fitter in one of our co-operatives. To hear him speak publicly or privately made one ashamed that we were not doing more for our country. He always denounced, in the most unmistakable terms, the greed and selfishness and indifference that was gripping Ireland and woe betide the person who would belittle my work or attribute the wrong motives in his presence. He has since died, but his daughter carries on in the same mould.

Then there was Bernie McGinley, handsome and full of humour, who has since married. Cool in demeanour but inwardly seething for progress. Completely unused to dealing with the public, yet evolving as the soothing trouble-shooter among customers from several nations. Always telling me where I was wrong, yet deeply loyal to me at all times. The product of a quiet country home, competent to take her place as a leader.

Mrs. Mary Anne Gillespie, interested intensely in progress, and irritated by slip-shod methods, always anxious that provision would be made for me if I became incapacitated. Noting the goal to be achieved, and unwaveringly seeking its achievement. Always ready to maintain her point of view, yet resilient enough to admit the validity of another's argument. Working now as manageress of the machine-knitting co-operative, and assisted by Mary O'Gara, she has placed the industry on a very successful course.

Finally, there was Francis Cunningham, the young headmaster of the school. He was ideally suited to community work for not only is he an excellent teacher but he was also a county councillor. Athletic, he is a very competent footballer and handballer, and played a very large part in the revitalisation and eventual eminence of the Glencolumbkille GAA. Perhaps more than any of us he knew the misunderstandings and the pitfalls that are part and parcel of the rural community. He is the most reticent of us all and inclined to bottle up problems and try to sort them out himself. I don't think I have ever seen a more indefatigable worker. Nothing was too hard for him and no hours too long, and his method of handling local criticism and false representation was, rightly or wrongly, silence.

Closely associated with us, shortly afterwards, has been Christina Daly, inheriting the intensely nationalist ideals of her father, outwardly cool, but inwardly seething with ideas, and deeply committed to making our little bit of Ireland a success.

And so in 1970 the Glencolumbkille Development Association was formed.

CHAPTER XIII

Just when all seemed to be coming to a standstill I had been joined by some remarkable people; and any community that produces their like is a good community. We resolved that we would forge ahead with future development as far as we could; that whatever we did would be done for the good of the community and not for personal gain; that we would borrow the capital from the banks and assume corporate responsibility in the repayment.

Our first action was to buy out my partner in the holiday village company. My fifty percent did not matter because it was donated to the Development Association anyhow. Our ownership of the holiday village provided useful collateral.

Then by a stroke of fate the local hotel came on the market. We were all convinced that we should not allow it to be bought by a foreigner. For nights on end we agonised over the acquisition of the capital. The bank would give us so much but not enough. Friends and well-wishers were approached for loans which they gave. Eventually we discovered that there was a shortfall of about six hundred pounds. This we made up by our own savings and borrowings.

We bought the hotel and thus had a firm tourist base established with it and the cottages. Of course the hotel was a natural social centre in the district because it was the only one for miles and for that reason it was traditionally kept open all the year round.

We tried to promote a free and easy atmosphere and gradually the people felt a certain proprietory sense because most of them knew that it was not being run for private profit. In the winter, we ran many dinner dances and I used to quip that the number of evening gowns in the district had jumped from single figures to several hundreds.

It was clear, however, that the demand for higher quality would eventually force us into expansion and modernisation. In this context we frequently discussed the possibility of building a large function room but we kept postponing it for lack of capital, which was a constant worry.

At this time I was a member of a social council established by the bishops. They held an annual conference each year in places like Kilkenny, Waterford, and Killarney. The conferences were attended by about two hundred people drawn from the voluntary and statutory bodies with speakers of international prominence.

At the August meeting, when the venue for the October conference was being decided I, as a good Northerner, intervened to suggest that some of the conferences should be held in the Northern half of the country, like Dundalk, Drogheda, Sligo or Letterkenny. Bishop Birch, the great social initiator in Kilkenny, who took a keen interest in us, intervened and said, "Why not in Glencolumbkille?". Immediately there was a ground-swell of assent for Glencolumbkille as a venue. I was aghast but I did not want to show the white feather, so I agreed. I knew we had enough accommodation between the hotel and the twenty tourist cottages, but we had no conference room.

I rushed home and met Francis Cunningham, and my first words were "Let there be a function room and it must be built within six weeks". Francis paled, and if he had not been a strong man, he would have sat down.

Never have I seen such intense activity. Land had to be excavated, springs had to be diverted, materials had to be bought, Bord Fáilte and planning authorities had to be consulted. Never before had the workmen of our parish shown such prowess for speed. Our own bishop arrived about two hours before the delegates. Everything was in chaos and the workmen were actually nailing on the back door. Being a wise man, the bishop went to a quiet room. I am sure he prayed. But the conference room was ready on time.

The hotel and its conference room were to provide the venue in 1977 for a more unusual conference. I was approached by a community worker from Belfast who asked me if I would host a conference from the Six Counties. As far as I could understand, the initiative came from the loyalist paramilitary group, the Ulster Defence Association (UDA), who selected Glencolumbkille as the venue for discussions between some of the prominent rival groups in the North.

At the time their reasoning seemed to be that the time had come for each faction to busy itself with the creation of some employment through its own initiative and on co-operative lines. Some had already begun such work on a small scale, and it was felt that there should be a sharing of experience.

I readily accepted the suggestion and a date was set; but I was warned that neither the gardaí nor anyone else was to be informed. Indeed, we kept the conference so secret that only two of us locally knew its purpose.

On the night the delegates arrived I gave them a welcoming talk. There were six representatives from the UDA, six Provisional IRA, six Official IRA, and — I think — six from the Ulster Volunteer Force; but in the circumstances I did not enquire about anyone's allegiances.

I opened the conference on the Saturday morning with an address telling the delegates that it was high time they stopped fighting each other, that they should instead build bridges between them and that this could be partially achieved by co-operation in job creation and by sharing experience in this field.

During their weekend in Glencolumbkille I was quite amused to observe the apparent comradeship and conviviality that developed between these men of such apparently different backgrounds. On the Saturday night I organised an Irish entertainment with local fiddlers and dancers. We sang Irish songs and Orange ballads, and the atmosphere was great. I wore an Aran sweater for the occasion, and this departure from the cloth seemed to put them more at ease. Indeed,

100

Sammy Smythe — press officer for the UDA — and I struck up a great rapport.

Later I was invited to Belfast and taken on a tour of inspection of the small co-operative ventures in which they were engaged and at night I addressed a cross-section of those involved and tried to offer them every possible encouragement. But it all passed; perhaps some good seeds were sown.

Sad to relate, Sammy Smythe was gunned down a few weeks after the conference.

As late as 1980 I attempted to forward a formula for peace; encouraged by my bishop, I approached Daithí O'Connell a leading member of Provisional Sinn Féin in Dublin, with a proposal which was the brainchild of Dermot Walsh, the Donegal hotelier. It started from the premise that the war in the Six Counties was a draw, that neither side could win and neither side could lose. O'Connell was interested, but he later informed me that he could not obtain the interest of those responsible in the North.

Over the years quite a number of ideas for creating wealth in the district occurred to me or were passed on to me; and each of these was checked out for feasibility. I was dissuaded from bee-farming because, although there was plenty of heather, there was too little clover. Noting the enormous amount of furze, or whins, I sent off samples to be analysed for perfume content, but this was too low to justify the manufacture of perfume. Even the making of chalk for sale to Irish schools was suggested, this time by an English well-wisher, but the Institute for Industrial Research and Standards advised me that the market was too limited to justify the cost of capitalisation.

Two French visitors suggested a way for speedy farming and harvesting of shellfish, but local people were not interested. The same two Frenchmen encouraged me to try snail farming and even offered to obtain a good market in France, but I did nothing about it when I was told that snails were low on reproductive capacity. Becoming interested in advanced duck-farming, I read all I could about it and then went to see a highly modernised duck farm in another county. But even though the owners gave me much useful information, they would not allow me to see the ducks; and I learned that the marketing of the birds could prove risky, and so was discouraged.

One of the most amusing incidents occurred when I became interested in mushroom farming. Off I went to Lough Gall in County Armagh in 1966 to find out all about it. There I was treated most courteously and as we visited one farm after another in this area of so many mushroom growers, I was certainly left in no doubt as to the great potential of mushrooms. The supervisor in Lough Gall, the late Jim McKiernan, actually offered to pick up our produce at the border if we took up production.

I considered that we had a ready-made base in our many derelict homesteads which, with their very thick walls could be easily insulated, and which were as large as some of the units in Lough Gall. I applied to the Department of Agriculture for more advice, especially on the making of compost, of which horse manure was considered a fairly vital ingredient. Two officials travelled all the way from Dublin, and were probably surprised to find me well informed. They concentrated on the weakest point of the scheme, which was the scarcity of horse manure; and in exasperation I pointed out that we had scores of donkeys, and surely their manure contained sufficient ammonia. At this they were rather disconcerted and had to confess that they did not know whether it did or not. They gave a noncommittal answer to my request that they have a laboratory test done, but said that they would be travelling to the Continent within a week to study an alternative method of making suitable compost.

They returned after a few weeks with an unenthusiastic report. "Tell me," said I, "did you have the donkey manure analysed?" They had not. "Well, if you do not report on this to me, I will arrive on the steps of the Department of Agriculture with some donkey manure in a cellophane bag and I will place it on the desk of the chief officer and instruct him to analyse it. Moreover, I will arrange to have an RTE camera present to record my carrying in this malodourous parcel." Needless to say, I did not carry out my threat; but the mere thought of it has entertained me with many a giggle since.

After the success of building the conference room, other problems began to assail us in Glencolumbkille. Our knitting factory, which had been depending on one outlet only for its product, gradually began to slip into a loss situation which the local shareholders were powerless to remedy.

Two major problems confront a rural co-operative generated and conducted locally: these are quality control and marketing. It is impossible quickly to generate skills in these areas. Messrs Pallas Ltd gave us very valuable help in quality control, and their insistence on top quality has left its mark on the performance of the factory since. But marketing proved a real problem because the price we were getting for our product left us too little margin for viable trading. After the first year the factory began to show a loss, and regardless of how much we produced the loss continued. Then in 1974 an independent audit commissioned by the Development Association disclosed that, technically, we were bankrupt. This was devastating news, for, if we declared bankruptcy, what would happen to the workers? We decided to close for a month, at the end of which our Development Association injected a few thousand pounds and we re-opened the factory ourselves and re-engaged our staff. The original shareholders and the Development Association, by its rescuing of the project from bankruptcy, ensured the permanence of more than twenty homes in the community and the circulation of about seventy thousand pounds per annum in wages.

We found that bringing in managers with experience and skills we felt we lacked was rarely satisfactory and in one case quite damaging. Indeed, our greatest success came with the development of individuals from within the community. Certainly, since we appointed Mrs Mary Anne Gillespie, a member of our Development Association, as manageress, the knitting factory has steadily gained in strength and has supplied work for thirty young men and women.

We divided responsibility among us for the hotel, the holiday village, the knitting factory and the folk museum. In every one of these enterprises we felt the pinch of inadequate capital, but nevertheless we were always open-handed in our subventions to any private entrepreneur whom we could entice into Glencolumbkille. This was done much to the chagrin of Gaeltarra Éireann who warned us time and again about this open-handed encouragement to private enterprise. They were right. The private enterprises which came to Glencolumbkille were a craft centre which we encouraged and established in the vacant Gaeltarra Éireann factory; a cut-and-sew enterprise in the old Teelin school; and a sportswear manufacturing unit in the Gaeltarra Éireann factory after the craft centre had collapsed. All these three enterprises failed, mainly because they were dependant on our Development Association for added subventions which we could not supply. It is difficult to refuse to help any private enterprise whether in crafts or in industry if you are hell-bent on full employment, but it is significant that the only enterprises of ours to survive were those which we controlled fully ourselves.

Our problem could be summed up thus: we were going too far too fast, without the back-up of adequate capital, and worst of all, there was a complete lack of local people willing or able to assume the responsibilities of management.

In 1976 I had reluctantly come to the conclusion that the best way to solve the problem was to sell our fixed assets before we got too old, and create a trust fund for the ongoing development of the community, in agriculture, industry, social welfare, and environmental protection. By 1979 there were only three of us who really belonged to the Development Association and we were responsible for a large complex of enterprises. Death and marriage had claimed the others, and as our respective avocations normally absorbed much of our time, the hours left each day for community development imposed an excessive strain. The hand-knitting co-operative was maintaining a steady output; the folk museum was constantly expanding, as was Errigal Eisc — originally the Errigal Vegetable Co-operative. The knitting factory was emerging from its difficulties, under the management of Mary Anne Gillespie who was applying new methods and developing new markets. The holiday village was maintaining steady business, as was the craft shop in Dublin, though this was suffering from heavy overheads. The hotel was being expanded and renovated and its new holiday village was completed; but it was carrying a very heavy overdraft. For some years I had been becoming more and more concerned about the future. What would happen if I, or any of us, was removed from the scene? Would people from the community step in and fill the vacant ranks? They surely knew that, even though the work and its profits were legally owned by us few, we were not laying claim to any personal profit. Nevertheless, no interest in continuity after our life span was ever evinced.

In the meantime, however, we had decided that if we were to keep pace with the requirements of modern tourists, we must expand and modernise the hotel. However, we could not possibly meet the capital cost involved. Consequently, we invited Gaeltarra Éireann to take up a minority holding in the hotel. This was done, but Gaeltarra Éireann insisted that all the holiday cottages be incorporated with the hotel in one company, to be called the Glenbay Hotel Company.

In deference to my contribution over the years, it was also decided by Gaeltarra Éireann that fifteen percent of the company's shares be allocated to me if and when I retired, because I was the only person who was not secured with an adequate pension on retirement. However, I have no plans to retire so I have refused the equity. It is also contrary to all our thinking that any member of the Development Association should derive personal gain from our community efforts. After my death, that fifteen percent equity will remain with the Association for future development.

The hotel was modernised and expanded and indeed it seemed that it would require very careful management for some years until the borrowed capital was repaid. To achieve this, we acquired professional management and advice with the intention of upgrading the tone of the hotel and increasing the turnover. These being the directors' top priorities at subsequent board meetings much time was devoted to them and conflicting approaches emerged.

The Association's representatives on the board were

anxious about the level of expenditure and what appeared to be a steadily worsening financial situation. But we were not professionals, not experienced in hotel management, and we deferred to advice which projected a large upturn in business and the elimination of financial difficulties with the trade of a reasonable tourist season.

But things went badly wrong. Never will I forget the sense of shame, mystification and hopelessness when the auditor announced in November 1980 that, during our past year's trading our debt had increased by £99,000. Turnover had virtually doubled but losses soared. In the year ended 31 August 1979, the turnover had been £137,818. In the twelve months up to August 1980, this rose to £271,790. But for the same two periods the loss before interest charges soared from £7,120 to £66,225, and after interest charges from £22,307 to £99,916. Even the income from food and entertainment fared remarkably badly (especially in the peak tourist season), showing respective losses of £31,833 and £13,900. This latter was our first ever experience of this because we had never before had an annual loss on entertainment, nor on food. More aggravating still was the disclosure that around £130,000 had been spent in cash transactions.

I just could not believe it, but the long line of unpaid creditors and the bank overdraft confirmed the stunning truth. I knew that this was the end of the road for further progress by our Development Association, for in no way could we repay this debt by normal trading.

The banks began pressing and the long list of creditors were restive. Liquidation was in the air but my colleagues and I were determined to stave off liquidation. In the midst of all our sorrow one good thing took place. We met the creditors and talked to the bank and they were all sympathetic and compassionate. Instead of going into liquidation it was agreed that we ourselves commence selling and repaying. That process has already begun and the conclusion to which I came some five years previously has now become a reality. We are gradually selling our separate assets. To add to our worries, the impression has been given in sections of the press that all our other, viable units have collapsed.

This trauma has not been as unbearable as I thought it would be for I have been sustained by another ideal. If we have money left after our sales, we intend to set up a trust for the adoption of a new "Glencolumbkille". But this time, "Glencolumbkille" will be thousands of miles away in the third world. These will be people who are in much greater need than we are in Ireland.

A light may be extinguished in Glencolumbkille, Ireland, but let us hope that a blaze will be ignited in another "Glencolumbkille" far away.

CHAPTER XIV

I am often asked "Was it worth while?" and "Would you do it all again?". The answer I give to the first question is "Look around!" and the answer I give to the second is "Gladly"! Many mistakes were made, but immeasurable success was attained both directly and indirectly. Insofar as I provided any leadership for the neglected, I can claim that there is now tangible progress, where before there had been the neglect of generations; there is now hope where there was apathy; there is now a growing, vibrant population where there was decline and gloom. And it was all achieved not by politicians or bureaucrats but by local people.

It is not always easy for people to admit that they have been propelled and stimulated by example, but at the local level, a private textile factory has been initiated by a man who trained in our factory. Several people have copied our holiday cottage scheme in one way or another, while others have benefited directly or indirectly by the opening of Glencolumbkille to tourist development. Our original vegetable processing factory gradually ushered in the concept of a fish processing factory which is now flourishing and thus, out of failure there was born success.

Even the still-born agricultural commune was succeeded by the Glencolumbkille hill farming scheme, which in turn gave way to the independent Glencolumbkille sheep farmers' co-operative which is of great benefit to local farmers. Our two principal industrial failures, where we flirted with private enterprise, left no-one jobless, for the redundant workers were absorbed into our other industries.

Nor was it in material progress alone that we made our impact. I think that the Glencolumbkille people *en masse*, and later, the small group who carried on, have dramatically underlined the practicality of community self-help, and its necessity especially for the neglected and underprivileged. People from other parts of Ireland, particularly along the Western seaboard are quite overt in their gratitude for the stimulation given by the Glencolumbkille effort in general, precisely because of its insistence on community independence. The ideas in tourist development which it helped to pioneer are found particularly useful. This has been gladdening to me because I never thought solely of Glencolumbkille. My philosophy was to throw down such a challenge that others in the world would pick it up and whilst avoiding our mistakes, would be inspired by our example, and surpass our efforts.

All my life I have been irritated by armchair critics and by theorists and bureaucrats, in the same way that I have been irritated by people who at meetings will indulge in destructive criticism, but will never venture anything constructive. As the saying goes: "the hurler on the ditch is always the best hurler".

My whole being cries out for action, moderated by the advice of colleagues and experts, of course. The compulsion to keep on doing something constructive within society has remained like a song in my heart. I have been engaged in a rebellion against paternalism and an assertion of the rights of communities to forge their own destinies. But now as I begin to yield some responsibilities within the Glencolumbkille base to others, I myself am tempted to ponder on scenes that are gone, on some of the pitfalls of community enterprise, and some of the dangers evolving in our disturbed world.

Before me there is a rotating montage of my experiences down the arches of the years — the fight for Irish freedom; the polyphony of the Maynooth choir; the day of ordination; the bombed rubble of London streets; the isolation of Tory island; the effortless gliding of a seabird over the cliffs of Sliabh Liag; the eager faces of audiences in many parts as they waited for a message of hope; the sleepless nights of

109

worry; the inimitable friendliness of the Irish people. And when the kaleidoscope of memories is stilled, I say to myself, "Glencolumbkille, I would walk your fields again".

We were unable to carry all the people of Glencolumbkille with us in our efforts but we were fortunate in being able to retain the absolute dedication of the few. This should not daunt anyone who is attempting an operation such as ours, for it is doubtful if any community in the world would ever become totally involved.

If I were to do it all again I would issue a weekly news bulletin where the written word would stand and there would be no opportunity for misunderstanding and misrepresentation. I would also retain an elected community council as I had for many years. This council would be elected annually, so that its critics could be given the opportunity of shouldering responsibility. Nevertheless, the election of such a council on an annual basis is not always the answer to change in personnel. Our elections were always held on the first day of January and a certain number of candidates were allotted to each *ceanntair* in proportion to population. All adults had a vote and a large proportion used it. But I did notice that some of the most vocal critics would not allow their names to go forward and the outgoing candidates — out of a sense of duty — accepted nomination time and again. Moreover, there is a danger that such a council would become a talking shop. A strong chairperson would ensure that resolutions were reached and progress reported.

It is my earnest wish, as private enterprise now takes over the tourist complex which we began, that they will continue its development in a manner which will not clash with the rugged surrounding environment, and that the visiting tourist will never be irritated by money-making gimmickry at every corner. It is sad to reflect that many tourist centres have been used for the exploitation of those who come to relax. Tourists do not holiday in a district in order to be harried. They like to have reasonably good entertainment which reflects the cultural tradition of the district, and most of them wish to be accepted by the local community.

But the world is becoming too highly urbanised. Modern

sophistication in the erection of urban housing too often gives rise to a life-style estranged from the real pulse of life. Women working in the home, the unemployed, and old people in institutions very often are crushed and extinguished by isolation and exclusion from participation in the shaping of our future.

Our young people cannot develop unless, at an early age, they have a sense of making a useful contribution and contact with a good range of people. Children have little opportunity to develop real self-respect and self-sufficiency if they are shut out of community activity, and herded within their own age groups too much of the time, or cut off from stimulus, alone with one beleagured parent in a dormitory suburb, watching the endless soul-destroying repetition of maintenance tasks.

I greatly treasure my experiences with young children. I do not know whether it is their absolute trust in the priest or their transparent innocence that has appealed most to me; but certainly as they crowd around and strive to get near me, I feel as if all my worries have fled. They seem to be at their best between the ages of four and ten; then there is a slight withdrawal when the cold hand of worldly wisdom begins to fall on their natural exuberance.

I set up a children's choir and a "Gaelic cabaret" with the local children; and on Sunday mornings after Mass they would come charging into the sacristy eager to receive a little pat or a hug and a word of praise. These few minutes with them easily outweighed the cares of the whole week.

For hours I would sit hearing their tensely whispered confessions of simple sins. Then in a voice of assumed solemnity I might ask, "Tell, me, child, when you were fighting did you win or did you lose?" In a moment the child would be suffused with giggles. The tension was broken. There surely must be no more rewarding experience than the bestowing on children not of presents, but love.

Children should be looked on as the adults of the future in a meaningful way — their education should include practical and creative contributions to their own community. Child care should be incorporated within sensible developments

111

undertaken by men and women and the very old — who do, after all, have much experience to offer. A little planning could combine child-minding with occupations for the old in a mutually beneficial setting.

Greater efforts must be made to halt the drift from rural areas — the population must be more evenly spread. A rural area should not depend on agriculture alone — it must also have sufficient industry to catch most of the redundancy from family farms.

Several small industries are preferable to one large industry, because the failure of one will not scatter the community. If there is complete dependence on one large industry then its failure can be ruinous. Small industries should, if possible, be locally owned and locally managed. No industry should be attempted unless the market projection for its product is guaranteed for at least one year in advance. Productivity may be important but quality of product is vital. Small industries cost the economy of the country much less per capita in job creation. Aloofness between management and workers begets estrangement and strikes. This is less likely in small industries.

The battle between labour and capital is inevitable in our society so long as workers have no control over what happens inside the place of work. If this running battle is not resolved soon, there is the danger that less democratic forms of control will emerge. Perhaps we should take a leaf out of the book opened by the Solidarity trade union movement in Poland, and extend democracy in industry so that workers can control their industries, and elect their managers.

Both sides of industry will have to make sacrifices. Certainly the investor must receive a fair return for money, but there must be a limit to the emolument of any person, no matter how competent or exalted he may be. In any given enterprise an agreement should be hammered out by the proprietors, the management and the workers which includes a ceiling for investors' gains and managers' salaries. But the workers should not be kept ignorant. Then, if the enterprise falls on bad times the workers will know that they cannot get blood out of a stone.

Where possible, in rural districts, industry should be built around local raw materials and traditional skills. If farms are small and uneconomic, then every effort should be made by local groups of farmers to combine them into an economic unit sufficiently large to give scope for mixed farming, then at least all the owners can be employed.

A moderately weak economy cannot afford the luxury of any of its citizens living above their means. Indeed, on a wider scale the world cannot afford to have anyone living in luxury. There is no room for any "Dives" in the world anymore: there are too many millions of the "Lazarus" variety.

In the perpetuation of this state of affairs the multi-national company will probably bear a greater and greater responsibility. Multinationals divide markets among them-selves in international cartels. Their total growth rate is twice as high as that of world production and it is estimated that by 1985 a comparatively small group of multinational companies will dominate eighty percent of the capitalist world's total industry.

The rationale of multinational capitalism which is more production and more consumption, does not necessarily generate the better life, because of its vast consumption of energy, raw material and capital. This vicious circle must be broken for if humanity becomes more and more dependent on highly organised but diminishing numbers of industries and institutions, then spontaneity and independence of choice will become sapped, and a point reached little better than subservience itself.

I do not think that we will see employment rise to the level of the early 'seventies again in our generation, because automation is marching on irresistibly. Millions of highly literate and enthusiastic young people are denied the oppor-tunity of work and our society may well live to regret this abandonment. Enthusiasm could be quickly supplanted by disillusionment, and disillusionment by drug addiction, and drug addiction by a wave of crime such as the world has never seen. It is extremely doubtful if our education of youth is the best possible. Too many of our young people have their ambitions set firmly on a job in one of the services. It is a safe job, but it does not directly produce wealth. It should be possible, in second-level education, to introduce much greater emphasis on business farming and business manufacturing. These two produce wealth and jobs. In business manufacturing the emphasis should be on small industry.

The co-operative concept outlined in these pages offers many solutions to the current crisis of unemployment. Only since the Industrial Revolution has there been such a splitting of "paid work" away from the rest of life. Many of the schemes outlined here show the integration of work with environment; the fruits of labours being retained by those who labour; the local natural resources employed; the integration of men, women, and children into enterprise that is both work and culture.

Such co-operative concepts allow for the old to make their contribution and to share benefits, avoiding the terrible neglect so many now face.

The time may well have come when the affluent West has reached saturation point in the purveying of its consumer products unless it makes an attack on world poverty and thus produces the climate for global trading on a fair and equal scale. If the area of reasonable prosperity is not broadened dramatically, and soon, then the ivory towers of the West will crumble and its economy will dip into decline.

It is certainly not beyond the powers of each sizeable company in the West, whether manufacturing or consumer, to adopt a community in the developing countries, not as a vassal but on equal terms.

All over the world there are billions of pounds being spent annually in the manufacture of weapons of destruction, and a sizeable proportion of the most competent people in the world are engaged therein. What is the reason that a supposedly civilised humankind should be engaged in this foolishness? It is certainly similar to the attitude of the cave-man except that it is more sophisticated. Is it due to fear or due to greed? If it is the former, then it is not beyond the competence of rational governments to meet and abjure all armaments except a standing army to protect its own society. If it is due to greed, then we are not yet civilised. It is in military rearmament that modern technology reaches its most sinister phase. For both in pollution and destruction, modern weaponry can obliterate all life on our planet many times over, and for centuries to come. How can countries be so influenced by rancour, greed, or fear, that a stock of weaponry can be assembled at the cost of some forty billion dollars a year while most of the world is groaning from malnutrition, illiteracy, and disease? In a very real sense this is money stolen from the poor and the sick on our planet. The education and life-work of at least four hundred thousand sophisticated experts and the wages and time of the producing workers are wasted, for their technological knowledge has one aim, and that is devastation.

These weapons experts must total approximately one-half of the Western world's team of researchers.

A mere five percent of the money devoted each year to military budgets would provide elementary education for seven hundred million children, or housing for three hundred million people, or food for two hundred million undernourished people. One nuclear submarine costs as much as keeping sixteen million children alive for a year.

The abolition of this vast expenditure on armaments could have a colossal effect on the creation of wealth-producing jobs at home, and if a sizeable proportion of this expenditure was devoted to the uplifting of the third world, then we would be witnesses to the greatest revolution the world has ever seen.

The threat of nuclear annihilation, and the coexistence of extreme poverty with conspicuous wealth must serve to emphasise that all humanity is one. The impulse that prompted my efforts in Glencolumbkille was not something which could only have developed there; somehow it would have found expression wherever I had been. Glencolumbkille was being bled to death by emigration and underdevelopment; it is now on its feet as a viable community, combining small farming, industry based on local materials, and tourism. While things did not develop as fully collectively, or communally, as I wish they might have, the major problems have been tackled and there is now relative prosperity.

115

Seeing how things now stand, and accepting that there is a lack of local anxiety and willingness to carry on the work, my thoughts have been turning in new directions. It seems clear to me that the great need to feed and clothe, to allow people to live their lives in dignity and independence, exists in Latin America, Africa and parts of Asia in far more pressing and immediate ways than it does in the Glencolumbkille of today. The means of communal enterprise — people taking it into their own hands to build human potential, to build for the future — are eminently applicable in the developing countries. If I can be of any use, I should like to assist such development.

Every nation should have the chance to strive to preserve its own identity and its own culture, for it is from the treasury of the vast variety of national cultures that the world is uplifted and enriched. There is a famine abroad in our world! True, in many countries it is a famine of bread, of learning, and of health. But more than anything else it is a global famine of people recognising their collective strength. In the field of politics there are few who follow principles rather than public opinion; and public men, instead of leading the masses by noble directions often lead them into ignoble ways. Our country's people are rendered too timid for individuality, too weak for heroism, and what is often true of politics is also true of religion.

And we need them to rise above mediocrity and we need them fast.

We need "ordinary" people to take power into their own hands and realise the greatness of collective effort. With the zeal of Christ burning within them, they would tear away the accumulated cobwebs of sophistry; they would confound our conventional morality with sincerity and they would let the stroke of their challenge ring on the massive shield of the world's hypocrisies and preach the lesson of justice on street corners. This is our greatest immediate need, and now.

Action! Action against injustice, inertia, hypocrisy and greed! It is for this that my whole being has yearned. In this I am moved by the old Irish mythological leader, Fionn MacCumhall, who instructed his harpist to play "not the music of things that are said, but the music of things that are done".

CALENDAR OF EVENTS

1910	Born in Kilraine, Glenties
1930	Entered Maynooth
1937	Ordained
1937	Curate in Wandsworth, London
1941	Curate in Orpington, Kent
1946	Curate in Brighton, Sussex
1947	Curate on Tory Island
1951	Curate in Glencolumbkille
1953	Community hall opened
	First agricultural and industrial show
1954	Community park purchased
	Electricity switched on
	First factory opened
1954-1960	Phased road improvements
1954-1963	Attempts to initiate new agricultural schemes
1956	First piped water scheme
	Feiseanna revived
1962	First co-operative factory opened
1962-1965	Lecture tours in West of Ireland
1963	Fund raising tours in United States and England
1964	Hand-knitting co-operative started
1964-1968	Group water schemes
1966	Knitting factory opened
1967	Folk museum opened
1968	Holiday village opened
1970	Development Association formed
	Craft shop opened in Dublin
1971	Hotel bought
	Moved to Carrick, as Parish Priest
1973	First extension to hotel
1978	Modernisation of hotel
1979	Hotel cottages built
1980	Decision taken to sell assets and create Trust Fund